UNDER BIG-HEARTED SKIES

UNDER BIG-HEARTED SKIES

*A Young Man's Memoir of
Adventure, Wilderness, & Love*

TOM STEWART

CANADA

Lucky Dollar Media
British Columbia, Canada
luckydollarmedia@gmail.com

Editor: Margo LaPierre
Proofreader: Brenna Davies
Page design, layout and typesetting:
Jan Westendorp/katodesignandphoto.com
Cover design: Serhat Özalp

ISBN 978-1-7772211-0-2 (softcover)
ISBN 978-1-7772211-1-9 (eBook)

"I'm convinced that there's something kind of timelessly vital and sacred about good writing. This thing doesn't have that much to do with talent. Talent's just an instrument. It's like having a pen that works instead of one that doesn't. [...] It seems like the big distinction between good art and so-so art lies somewhere in the art's heart's purpose, the agenda of the consciousness behind the text. It's got something to do with love. With having the discipline to talk out of the part of yourself that can love instead of the part that just wants to be loved. Really good work probably comes out of a willingness to disclose yourself, open yourself up in spiritual and emotional ways that risk making you look banal or melodramatic or naive or unhip or sappy, and to ask the reader really to feel something. To be willing to sort of die in order to move the reader, somehow. Even now I'm scared about how sappy this'll look in print, saying this. And the effort actually to do it, not just talk about it, requires a kind of courage I don't seem to have yet."

— DAVID FOSTER WALLACE

To Diane and Don Stewart

AUTHOR'S NOTE

THERE ARE TWO PARTS TO THIS MEMOIR. *BOOK ONE: Summers at Sabourin* spans six summers working in Northern Ontario starting when I had just finished high school. *Book Two: Boyhood and Onwards* begins with me as a young boy and ends with me in my early thirties. If both were combined, Sabourin would fit in the middle. But those stories are set in the same location, do well read together, so they're collected up front. I'd start there.

In the stories that follow some names have been changed.

CONTENTS

BOOK ONE: SUMMERS AT SABOURIN

BOOK TWO: BOYHOOD AND ONWARDS

BOOK ONE

SUMMERS AT SABOURIN

INTRODUCTION TO SABOURIN

WHAT FOLLOWS ARE TRUE STORIES FROM LONG-PAST summers working at the isolated Sabourin Lake Lodge as a fishing guide and shore-hand. It was a unique time and place, and things have changed now so it won't be repeated.

When the season ramped up to full, there were about twenty guides, and for descriptive brevity, they were of two groups: the Natives and the White Boys. The Natives made up about fifteen to twenty of those numbers on any given year, and the White Boys the rest. In my eyes, people are human beings first and whatever group they might consider themselves belonging to—be that tribe or country or religion or race—second. I'll understand if you disagree with that. This particular group of people called themselves Natives, sometimes Indian, and told me to do the same. Years later someone else not of that heritage let me know the correct term was *Aboriginal*. Years after that I was told it was *First Nations*. Back then if I had called these guys Aboriginal to their faces, they'd have either laughed at me or called me a racist—I never once heard them use either of those terms in my six years working with them. I'll call anyone whatever they want but it was Natives to *them,* so respectfully, that's the word I'm using in these stories from their time. They were all over forty, some over sixty, and all had worked as fishing guides for decades. Many of their pasts included residential schools, troubled families, tough areas of Winnipeg or the reserves of Manitoba and Ontario. Alcohol was a dark thing in most of their stories. Most had spent some time in jail, some of them for serious crimes, a few for homicide.

As for the White Boys, two years before I arrived there were none. The year I left we were five. I've heard today, fourteen years later, there are just four or five Natives, First Nations, guiding there now.

It's worth saying now in case it appears otherwise that there really wasn't much racism up at Sabourin, or if there was it wasn't so obvious to me. Sometimes in their own languages the Ojibwe would slur the Cree, and the Cree would slur the Ojibwe. But that was rare and they usually both just spoke English or sometimes an intersectional language called Oji-Cree. When they did that, all the Natives there could understand and nobody else. Sometimes they would do that when we all sat for breakfast or dinner together, and then they'd all laugh. Sometimes a few of the Natives would give the White Boys a hard time, and sometimes a couple of the White

Boys would take a shot at a Native when he wasn't there. But most of the time everyone just got along, and if there were any conflicts it was almost always between individuals. I use the terms "the Natives" and "the White Boys" fondly. My memories from six years with these characters are all bits of gold and all is cherished, and all is forgiven, and I could only hope the same for me. It was a group of people from different backgrounds, but we were all of us mostly similar. In my fourth year I found out second-hand that they had nicknamed me "the Blonde Indian." They liked to laugh a lot. We all did.

SABOURIN

Sabourin Lake Lodge in Northern Ontario was accessible by float plane only. You flew from either Selkirk, Manitoba, a short drive from where I grew up, or Red Lake, Ontario, which during the 1930s was the busiest airport in the world, servicing the gold mines in the area. The wilderness surrounding Sabourin Lake was made up of old forest with moose, bear, wolf, beaver, mink, marten, fox, eagles, and it was still trapped in the winter. Sabourin Lake gave access to dozens of other lakes, all that we fished, all via the Bloodvein River. It had been a fishing lodge since 1959, and in 2000 I turned seventeen years old and would spend four months a year for six summers there. For a Manitoba boy who grew up in love with fishing and the woods and old stories of hunters and trappers, there was no other place I'd rather be.

The lodge itself was constructed from trees felled onsite, built on a hill, and had twenty-foot-high picture windows that overlooked the big lake. A couple dozen log cabins sprawled out and away from the lodge to house guests and staff. The lodge had a towering stone fireplace and chimney, pool table, trophy fish on mounts, and separate dining areas for staff and guests. Old photos hung on the walls showed people standing on either side of a long stringer, the large fish hanging in the middle. But that old-world practice changed about the time I arrived, and it became catch-and-release everything except what was kept for shore-lunch. The numbers of fish and big fish rebounded.

The guests were almost entirely wealthy American men on a mix of vacation and corporate trips. There were even a few groups that had been coming for decades and over generations. There was Southern oil money, company founders, lawyers, doctors, CEOs, and managers of large companies that sometimes brought up employees rewarded for meeting incentives. I knew of at least two billionaires. No large group of people can be generalized. There are too many differences of integrity and values among its members for any meaningful claim to be true. Money or power or the lack thereof doesn't define a person's character. I've met the arrogant poor and the humble rich. I don't see an honesty in being poor or dishonesty in not being. There are people with money that spend modestly and write their wills to give it all away, who volunteer, are good parents and friends, and vote their conscience. Some people are just lucky to be born into a good family and go to a good school and that shouldn't come with guilt, because they didn't choose it. I thought that if

I couldn't use wealth or title or race or tribe to infer a person's character, and given that any one person from any group could share my values of tolerance and decency and opportunity and kindness, I would try to keep an open mind towards everyone I met, both guests and guides alike. I chose to try to give people the benefit of the doubt. Sometimes I didn't do it as well as I would have liked to.

In early and cool mornings the guide boats would leave the docks and pick up the guests from the sand beach in front of their cabins, the chimneys smoking. A guide and two guests in a boat for the day, three or four days of fishing before the next group arrived. If a big group had travelled to Sabourin together, then the whole party with all their boats would meet up for shore-lunch somewhere out on the lakes. If you made that trip to Sabourin, which for some was three plane rides from home, not cheap, and landed you to a place entirely different from the one you left, you were always happy to be there regardless of the weather or the fishing. And I felt the same during my time spent working there.

With my two guests in front, we'd cruise out on sunrise waters to our choice of dozens of lakes, hundreds of square kilometres we could fish. I'd breathe in a mix of cold Northern Canadian lake air, forest smells, and sometimes cigar smoke—and love all of it.

FRED THE BOSS

FRED WAS ABOUT FIVE FOOT THREE, FIFTY, AND ONE hundred and sixty pounds. He first started working at Sabourin Lake Lodge in the 70s. The polio from his youth meant he walked slowly with a limp from the metal brace and had pain. He wouldn't tell you about the pain. He was the boss: tough, smart like a physicist, practical like a farmer, kind, forgiving, funny. A unique human.

His talents extended to the cuss and he could swear with an artistic creativity like few ever heard. A mixture of sacred religious reference, female body parts, and new takes on old classics like *shit* and *damn*—profanity's bread and butter. His muse could be anything. I'd hear him from under the lodge where a copper water pipe froze in the spring and broke before sunrise, the ground cold, freezing water running down his neck while trying to solder in the dark. Or if a late afternoon float plane unexpectedly arrived with a drunk fishing guide from another lodge, whose pockets were freshly padded with US cash, coming to take our cook—his lover—away mid-season, Fred would string something wonderful together. He was a great storyteller and armchair philosopher, and on coffee breaks or working alongside him, it was a pleasure to listen.

Servicing of the generators, boats, and tractors, as well as all general upgrades and repairs electrical, mechanical, plumbing, and carpentry, were Fred's departments. And together he and his wife, Susan, catered to all the guests in the evenings; scheduled the daily multiple float plane trips; and managed all the forty staff, a task made more challenging by the unique complexities of isolated camp life.

Twenty years before I arrived, Fred disassembled an old excavator tractor in Red Lake, had those individual parts flown up in a Beaver, then reassembled it piece by piece. One fall, after all the guests and the other guides had left, he and I and another guy stayed on to dig in a new septic system. While digging with the tractor bucket in the afternoon, the weight of a load pushed a sharp snapped root through a tire with a loud bang. We were also getting low on hydraulic fluid and grease. You can't just fly off to the nearest town half an hour away for supplies if that flight itself costs a thousand dollars. And that's why Fred was there. He unbolted that big four-foot-high tractor tire and laid several fibreglass patches on the inside against the rubber, sealing the hole. Then he filled the hydraulic oil tank with canola oil and packed a grease gun with Crisco lard. When we got back to work and that backhoe warmed to operating temperature, it smelled delicious and worked fine.

At close of day another season, I was returning from the lakes in my boat with a pair of guests. We watched Fred walk down the beach to greet us as he sometimes did to hear about the day of fishing. One of the guests turned to me and asked what Fred's handicap was. I sat there dumbfounded, confused, not knowing how to answer. In my eyes he was the exact opposite of that word. After dropping them off, I cruised slowly back to the docks. I genuinely didn't even figure out what the guy meant until I was walking away from my boat.

PAUL FOX AND THE LITTLE RABBIT

WHEN I HAD ONLY JUST ARRIVED TO SABOURIN AND IN
my first week of my first year, I was shooting a pellet gun
in the evening after work. Paul Fox, forty, one of the bigger Natives pushing three hundred pounds, said to me,
"If you see that rabbit I'd love to take some home at the end
of the year. I'll freeze him if you get him." And not long
after I did see the cottontail and he wasn't concerned at
all with how close I was. I laid the space between his eye
and his ear on the open sights.

As a kid growing up in rural Manitoba, I had shot and
snared a lot of rabbits. I'd skin some, make soup, sometimes BBQ them or cook them buried under coals of a fire
my dad allowed me to make in the backyard. One time
my mom came home from work, opened the fridge, and
found a tupperware labelled *Bunny*—she still laughs at
that.

This one was a dead thing where he now sat, and my
finger rested on the trigger. I watched him nibbling clover. I paused. For no intelligible reason, I just did not feel
like shooting that one that day. My finger unbent and the

gun lowered, this little rabbit continued nibbling on the clover, oblivious to how close he was.

A few days later, I casually told Fred I saw a cottontail around the work shed. And he says, "If you'd had shot that rabbit we'd have packed your bags, flown you out, and you'd be done here. It arrived the same day the trapper of this area, Bill Perrault, died. The Natives say it's him. They would have skinned you alive." And so two little animals got lucky that day. Later on I thought to myself, I should tell Paul so he doesn't accidentally shoot that rabbit either.

It was mid-summer and so far I'd only been working onshore, helping around the docks, learning some carpentry and plumbing and trades with Fred. I liked the work but I wanted to guide. I was obsessed with fishing and loved the water. I'd been allowed to take the odd guest out fishing for a couple hours in the evenings, but I was still learning and hadn't been given a whole day yet.

And then one afternoon Fred came up to me. "We're putting you on the lake tomorrow. Is there anyone you want to guide with for your first time out?" I was thinking, *Not the other White Boy. I like Johnny Moore and Stanford Paishke. I like Joe and Alex Quoquot, but they don't say much. I like Isaac Abraham, but he might get us lost . . .* "Paul Fox."

Fred stared at me.

"Yeah, Paul if that works. He's been pretty nice."

Fred continued staring at me. "All right then," he finally said.

I was pumped. My first full day guiding: taking out guests at sunrise, fishing until shore-lunch, fishing the afternoon, coming back for dinner. I found Paul and told him we'd been paired up together.

"Okay. I'll show you how to make the best fish." He took my printout paper map and marked where we'd meet up for shore-lunch with a big "X." It was a forty-five-minute drive away with lots of twists and turns and narrow spots out to Larus Lake. I'd never been there before, it wasn't that popular. "Here. We'll meet here at noon. You can't miss it. In a big bay. After lunch we'll drive together and I'll show you Larus Falls close by. The guests'll like that."

"Okay. Thanks, Paul." Pumped.

My boat was clean and ready to go, but I cleaned it again anyway and made sure I had all my gear: cast iron pan and spatula I'd never used, full gas, net, pliers. Everything looked good.

It was a bluebird-beautiful morning, like most of them up there, and I headed to the lodge and ordered my usual breakfast: one egg over easy, toast, sausages, one pancake, tea. I got that every day to the point the cook named it "the Tom," and for years others ordered it by name. That morning I'm a guide eating with other guides.

I walked down to the docks, the long lengths of two docks with twenty boats between and in their slips, where guides like me were coming and going with their gear. Motors were being started and idled warm. Their exhaust without wind to stir hung on the water in low clouds.

I started mine, carefully backed out of the slip, forwards between the docks, then turned towards the beach nearby. My two guests stood on the sand with their poles and cooler. We loaded the boat and headed out.

Instead of driving out to Larus in one go, my guests and I fished our way there slowly, stopping and trying different spots along the way as I fingered our course on the map. We found walleye, we hit no rocks: this is a happy boat.

For our last spot of the morning, I had us jigging close to the bay marked with the "X" so I could watch Paul come in and follow him to shore.

It's noon: *No rush—we're fishing not banking.* Twelve-fifteen: *That's barely different than twelve.* Twelve-thirty: *C'mon Pauly baby, would be nice if you cruised in now.* Twelve-forty-five: *What would I do first, the filleting? The fire? How long do they actually cook?* One o'clock: *All right, then.*

I pulled out my map again: I did not get it wrong. The "X" was on the map. It was in a big bay. You could see the pile of wood by a rusted forty-five-gallon drum cut in two and laid lengthwise. Larus Falls was on the map not far away. One hundred percent, this was the spot.

We idled in and unloaded.

"Maybe they turned around or hit a rock. It happens. But it's okay, I'm going to make you guys lunch and then I'll take you to this most beautiful set of falls. You get to catch up with your party when we're all back at the lodge this evening." They knew it was my first time out and smiled to my pitch.

I went about the work. The result was fillets that looked like a blind man took a butter knife to them; both the fish and potatoes were edible but soggy from oil too far from its smoking point; the cans of beans and corn in a pail of water over the fire heated but not long enough and were served lukewarm. My guests ate some from a mixture of courtesy and hunger, and the rest fed the gulls.

Larus Falls wasn't far and we set out for it. We navigated a section of river, then rounded a bend where the channel widened out to a lake with churning white froth at the other end. Cruising, the distance closed, and next to the falls there shone the glint from sun on an aluminum hull. *Paul's*. We tied the bow line to an aspen overhanging the water. My guests headed one way to find their friends by the rapids. I went the other to where Paul was packing up his cooking gear.

As I approached he saw me coming, and he neither greeted nor acknowledged me.

"You told me after lunch. I have the map here. The 'X.'"

"What? I said the falls." I go up to him. Right up to him. I step in his way and block the path back to his boat. He's big and wide with a big wide head. In weight, he's an honest two young Toms. Paul stares at me, his cast iron pan in one hand. I stare back.

I can't say I thought that decision through. I was pissed off and my adrenaline was pumping and that's about it. This will sound like clichéd bravado and so be it: sometimes you want to take a stand for what you believe in. And me at seventeen believed that being lied to by someone you trusted and thought liked you, someone you hoped was going to teach you, was worth pushing back against. And even today, I wouldn't tell him he's wrong. But it's complicated. At that moment as a young man I didn't take into account what Paul's upbringing might have been like and how people might have treated him. I don't know what his particular story was but I know for a fact a lot of those guys I worked with had rough ones. And if you're going to weigh all the pieces on whether to call someone out, that should get taken into account. I'm not sure what I'd say to younger me right then. He and I might not even speak the same language anymore. With time you end up calling things by different names or using the same names for different things. What you see as courage or strength or sacrifice or valour or beauty are subject to change over your life. They might still be changing for me. Over time they can look a lot different. He might have thought he was hearing one thing when it meant the other. He might have bought into some sort of folksy respectability of a cowboy or good ol' boy or hockey-fight ethic—the charm of settling things with a fist fight peaks when you're about seventeen years old. And I'm not saying there's nothing to it: you get those feelings out instead of harbouring them, you take a stand for what you believe in, you try to settle it and move on. That's not entirely bullshit. It's not necessarily toxic masculinity or whatever people want to label it. I might tell my younger self: It's your call as long as you've thought about the consequences 'cause sometimes people fall back and hit their head and there're some things you can't take back. Sometimes people even go to jail for it—not often but you open yourself up to that chance. The movies just show a sore fist or jaw and the respect earned—and respect is something to a young man. It's not nothing to an older one. It's complicated. I don't know what's right there and I don't know what I'd tell him. And knowing him, he probably wouldn't listen anyway.

It's me and Paul stood off. For a few seconds, each the other's world entire. Then he looks away. Not down. Just away. And then he steps off the path around where I stood and walks to his boat.

He could have been humouring my existence the way you might not step on a sidewalk ant. He could have been on probation. He could have thought swinging would end his season early. It could have been cowardice. I didn't know then and I don't know now.

I told my guests nothing about it and we fished out the afternoon for northern pike, then slowly returned our way home. After dropping them off in front of their cabin and putting my boat back in its slip, I hadn't cooled down much and went to look for Fred.

And Fred's laughing. And Fred's smiling. And he kindly says, "You just make sure you got yourself taken care of."

IF YOU WERE INDIAN

LES JAMES WAS THE HEAD GUIDE. SUNKEN EYES SHADED in dark sockets. Shoulders and neck like a bull. Top heavy, big forehead, deep voice, smart, a natural leader. His hat sat high on his head and read *Native Pride*. He intimidated more of the White Boys than all the other older guides combined, though Paul Fox was bigger. But there was a difference between Paul and Les. Les had a code of conduct, and that made him respectable, a consistency to his sense of justice, even if you were at the other end of it. Les might kick your ass over something trivial, but he wouldn't lie or steal or cheat you. There was even some sort of draw to him—you wanted him to like you. I did, anyway.

That first summer I was seventeen, five foot ten, about one hundred and fifty pounds. It was Les's cousin Bob, forty, six foot two and an honest three hundred, who grabbed me from behind and tried to throw me off the dock in the morning for some minor disrespect I had showed him the night before. I got low and scrambled, he lost his grip, and I backed away down the dock. Shortly after, I noticed Bob had broken the gold chain around my neck. So I went up to him. "You're paying for this." He swung hard and landed a large pair of pliers upside my head. Temple. It rang but didn't draw blood. I told him he was fucking crazy. In the emotion of it, I went and told Fred up at the office of the lodge. When I started telling it, I cried—seventeen and still couldn't help it.

There were occasions as a kid I didn't want to cry but couldn't hold the tears back. Not often, but a few times a year over the years. I wanted to be able to control my emotions or at least constrain the revealing of them for a time of my convenience—my image of a tough guy or something. Who knows where that value comes from. Maybe movies or other kids at the playground. Maybe it's just evolution because showing weakness makes you look vulnerable and that could open you up to something trying to eat you, or in the least, take away your banana. I don't think it's necessarily a bad thing to want some control there. Of course, that can run you into problems if everything gets bottled up for too long. When I couldn't help the tears, there was a bit of self-imposed shame about it. Growing up, some guys want to be cowboys but they're heart-on-their-sleeves kind of guys, I guess.

Anyways, that same morning, Fred had Bob flown out of camp. (He would be back next year though. Everybody gets forgiven at Sabourin.) On his way to the float plane with his bag packed, he walked by and he said to me, and he's smiling just a bit when he says it, "Somebody from IP will come see you this winter. Won't be me, but someone will." That's Indian Posse. I was away that winter anyways.

Because I brought it to the boss I guess I was marked a rat—some of us came from different schools. A few days later, Big Bad Les, you said to me, "If you were Indian, we'd have killed you."

A week passed and I was walking to the docks on the sand path under pines: the lake to my right, forest to my left, the docks ahead, and the lodge behind. I see you coming and it's just us and there's nowhere to turn off without running away like a scared little rabbit. I was sure I was going to take a beating there. I remember this like I'm looking through glass. You don't eyeball the man you're wary of, and so as our distance closes, I keep my face calm, eyes ahead and averted from yours—but I assure you every other single particle in me was supercharged to your presence. If people have auras, right then I'd have lit a city. We're down to our last steps on the narrow path, and as we approach, you feint me—you fake lunge. I jump like a scared little rabbit. You hack a couple deep slow laughs and keep walking.

There were some tense times that year but things cooled down and next season came. I wasn't at the docks that morning and I'm not sure exactly what that new kid did. A shore-lunch pail missing flour, music too loud, a hat backwards—something trivial. They said you held him by his neck in front of everyone in the back of one of the boats. I saw his bashed-up eye black for a week. *Les.*

A few boat motors were still two-stroke and hard to pull-start in the cold mornings. Sometimes they flooded out in the process. It was a windless sun-risen morning and Les was bent over one of those Mercuries tearing at the pullcord with big right hands for all of ten minutes. The motor making a lifeless, throaty gurgle. The boat rocking side to side on the calm water. A few of us watching. I'll bet you knew we were watching—I never thought about that until now. That summer you smacked around Jordan too. *Les James.*

Another season passed. I'd never be his size, but he was into his forties with a lot of years of heavy drinking and hard winters on the reserve. I filled out a bit, not much, but some. I was in the work shed sharpening a chainsaw blade with a file mid-morning. He came into the tight quarters, saw me and started bitching, "White boys never fucking carrying their load. Not pulling their fucking share around here."

Bullshit, I thought. I worked my ass off every day onshore when I wasn't guiding. Some of the other White Boys didn't, but neither did some of the Natives. When Les got all worked up he yelled and had spit on his lips and he spat on the ground and his eyes opened wide. "I'm always working," I said. I wasn't sure what was going to happen there.

Fred was our boss but he and I liked each other like good friends do. After six years of seeing him problem-solve, handle people, and hearing how he thought about things, I learned a lot from him. That same day at coffee break, I told him how Les was chewing me out—not to tattle, just for conversation. He says to me, "You could probably take him." I shit you not. He said something like this to me, "One of you guys could stand up to him."

I said, "Maybe Jordan."

I went about the day working, but my mind was churning away. That little comment blew up in my head like a prairie storm.

The kitchen table in the lodge is where all of us ate dinner, a ways up the hill from the docks and cabins. Every evening, everyone came up the hill to eat. I was sitting on the steps out front of the kitchen door.

"Coming in to eat?" some asked as they pass me.

"Soon," I said.

I was watching who had come up that night. Most had. Les hadn't.

And there he is. My heart is pounding. Even now all the years later. His big head and big shoulders the first things rising up the hill. I stand up and walk towards him. Everything feels a bit surreal. I don't walk too far, I want this close to the kitchen—I want people to come out and pull him off me if I'm losing. He sees me walking towards him, straight to him. I was surprised he knew my intention 'cause he said with a grin, "Heyyyy White boyyyy." That's what he said.

I had a knife on my belt in its sheath. I took it out so he could see me do it, and I tossed it away from us—he might've had one and I wanted him to know I threw mine away. He'd know how to use one.

I say, "I'm tired of your racist bullshit. Let's go." That's it. If I was going to make this up, those lines would be better.

We squared off. I'd been in a couple fights before but didn't really know what I was doing. It's just us out there looking at each other over two sets of clenched fists. I knew beforehand I was outgunned, then when I saw his head movement, his eyes on my shoulders and hands, not returning my stare, I knew I was outclassed too.

Fuck it just be first just get one in, I told myself. I threw a wide and my hardest right hand. That's not a good opening shot but that's what I did. *I fucking drilled him*: side of the head, temple, and ear. He seemed rattled and I was surprised. I threw the exact same punch again. He put up his left, partially blocked it, but it carried through enough. He stammered then tripped and fell. Les covered up quickly on the ground expecting a kick. I yelled at him, "Get up!" He's up, then we were both on the ground and I'm not sure how. I think he rushed me. We were scrambling away on the ground and the hard sand dusted up.

I didn't hear them come out of the kitchen, but I knew there was a crowd around us now, and even while fighting I could hear Fred say, "Hold on. Let it go a bit." We were both trying to get position and get on top of the other, trading little jabs without much weight behind them as we were scrapping away. Then Fred said, "Okay." And James and Jordan grabbed us, separated us. And we're up. I see blood by his ear. My shirt is ripped and mostly off. We're both dusted up from the hard sand, and panting.

Fred says, "What started this?"

I'm a little surprised and pause at that question right then because, Fred, you kinda knew that answer. But I say, "He's always threatening, saying we're not pulling our share. He's a bully. He's just fucking racist."

And then Les yells, "That's how I was raised!"

I hold on to those words. Right now, too. They're honest and they're telling: we're genes and upbringing and environment and ultimately nothing's really anyone's fault and so we're all forgiven. But right then I was twenty years old and coursing with adrenaline and there was a crowd around us, and even though I didn't hate Les, and I didn't like the feeling of fighting, I look in his eyes and I say, with Jordan and James and Fred and that kid and everyone else standing around, I make myself say and try to sound like I mean it, "Then get fucking used to this."

That's it. It ended there. As the crowd broke up and I turned to walk for my cabin and go clean up and change for dinner, I heard someone say, "Man, that was inspiring." I heard them say it was inspiring.

A couple days later I was at the docks in the morning talking to Stanford to find out where to meet up for shorelunch. He tells me. I look over at Les in the boat next to him. Les says something to me about the weather. And I agreed.

———

I grew up in the rural municipality of St. Andrews, Manitoba, in a middle-class family with parents that stayed together. I saw love, felt it, gave it. I could play any sport or instrument I wanted to. I could play safely outside all day or walk down the street to the Red River to fish. I never saw racism, or if I did I didn't recognize it at the time. I rarely saw poverty. I've read that it's not racism if a minority group is prejudiced against a majority group. It's been said to me it was not possible for Les to have been racist to the White Boys. All right. He was hard on us because we were White boys and admitted to that fact. Tell me the word for that and I'll use it. And maybe it does need its own word because it's not systemic generational prejudice where most of one's ancestors died of smallpox brought by invading colonialists who then exploited the Indigenous peoples and their land and sent

28

a lot of their kids to residential schools where they suffered abuses and sometimes died. That's a horrendously sad history. I can't empathize with those that suffered it. I'm not trying to diminish its horror. But I didn't do that to Les or his ancestors. And I don't have guilt for something I didn't do, wasn't alive when it happened. I'm not apologizing or feeling guilty for a lucky upbringing. I became friends with a lot of those Natives up there and most of them judged me only by my actions and that's how I judged them. I don't exactly know why they nicknamed me the Blonde Indian, but when I found that out I glowed the rest of the day. I walked taller. It's a fond memory and a nice thing and I choke up now writing it. If anyone would laugh at it, let them. Like I said, we mostly just got along up there in the summers in Northern Ontario because we had a lot more in common than just fishing. But we had that too.

STANFORD

ONE SUMMER IN THE EARLY 1980S, NEARLY TWO DEC-
ADES before I arrived, a stretch of bookings was coming
up where the lodge would be short a guide. Fred and a
pilot got in the float plane and flew for Red Lake, twenty
minutes away, to recruit. When they got there, Fred went
straight to the only bar in town. And that afternoon,
there sat eighteen-year-old Stanford Paishke. Fred propositioned him a guiding job at Sabourin, and Stanford
accepted and would go on to return every summer for
decades to come. When I arrived and when I left, Stanford
was the longest-serving guide and the best guide.

Stanford had big glasses, missing teeth, shoulder-
length and scraggly black hair with patches of bare scalp.
He was pleasant and agreeable when sober. He and his
wife, Mary, would sometimes get into it over the winter.
One winter she stabbed him but he survived.

Some of the long-time American guests would only
come if they could be guided by him, would make
their schedules based on his availability, and would
tip him thousands of US dollars at the end of their stay.

Occasionally, Stanford would be invited to the guests' lounge after the day was over for a game of chess. The highly educated clientele, some of them CEOs of well-known companies, would sit across from this run-down-looking figure, the chess pieces stood between them. Stanford, a couple Labatt Blues in by now, would proceed to hand them their asses. He was in his own class for finding trophy-sized walleye hiding on the bottom of those lakes. He could cite obscure baseball stats for players of current and former times. And if you sat across from him at the chess table, he would ruin you.

I grew up north of Winnipeg. With my family, we would drive the twenty minutes into the city for things we couldn't get in our area. Sometimes we'd go to Garden City Mall for clothes or prescription glasses. I remember that at one end of the mall, in the middle of the walkway and between the stores, there was a big chessboard tiled into the floor, its pawns and kings three feet tall, the same size I was. People were still allowed to smoke indoors back then and the smoke hung over the area where they played and sat and stood and watched. My mom would hold my hand when we walked by. Stanford told me that he used to play there sometimes.

The Canadian government implemented the residential school system in the 1880s, though its origins went further back than that. It took many First Nations children from their homes, and among other things, tried to make White children out of them. The residential school system was administered by Christian churches and caused a lot of harm and still does, well past the day in 1996 when the last school closed. The worst acts possible are those carried out on children, and the residential schools were rampant with abuses "physical, sexual, emotional, and psychological."[1] The odds of dying in those schools were higher than fighting in the Second World War.[2]

Stanford, like some of the other guides, was raised in those schools. And in one particular year and while I knew him, he received a settlement from a class-action lawsuit filed against the Canadian government. It's not my place to comment on the decision to give settlement money to a person with alcohol and drug addictions. And not everyone that attended those residential schools ended up with addictions. I just knew some that did. Stanford used his payout to buy a lot of cheap liquor and shortly thereafter I attended his funeral.

THE BEAVER DAM

ONE MORNING AT COFFEE BREAK, FRED TOLD A STORY of jumping a beaver dam in a boat: it could be done, he'd done it. James and I exchanged glances. "Back in the 80s," Fred said, "the motors were two-stroke and much lighter than the four-stroke Hondas that replaced them." James and I paid little attention to that comment.

And so that evening we hashed it out. Besides puncturing the hull, ripping off a skag, seriously hurting ourselves, or getting fired, we didn't see the harm in trying. It was agreed on which particular dam gave us the best chance for success: a thirty-minute cruise out on the Blood vein River. It dammed a creek that was wide and long enough on the other side to serve as a landing strip for a small boat.

After work the following day, we went to *James's* boat and took out the fishing gear and frying pans and all the other excess weight except the plywood-box car stereo we had made and two Labatt Blues. Our wake in the harbour.

We arrived to the tangle of sticks and logs that was some unsuspecting and large rodent's home we hoped to ram at full speed to send us airborne. Where the dam met the water's edge, there was a softened and sloping mud bank that seemed fortuitously well suited as a launch ramp. James and I picked over the water that shallowed to the shore for boulders and logs, the dam for protruding sticks, and having done so, felt satisfied that this seemed minorly less stupid now. We crawled down off the dam and into the boat. We shoved off. We turned and drove a hundred feet away. After a couple trial runs, James felt he had the timing down: at the last moment, tilt the motor up at full speed; hit the kill switch while the propeller spins through the air at full RPM; hold the motor in position while bracing for flight. I sat midway in the boat as general counsel and dead weight. *The next run would be live.*

We had a final safety briefing and pep talk before I put the Fatboy Slim CD in the car stereo. I hit play. We looked into each other's eyes. "Go time, buddy." James cranked the tiller throttle to full. Twenty-five horsepower might not sound like much, but when the boat is twelve feet of thin aluminum—it is. Our wake spread out behind us, lily pads blurred past us: we sped towards a wooden wall.

It was short time to this nickel-critter's home, and the last thing I saw was that perfect little mud ramp. Our boat's keel made contact at full speed, *and we launched.* I heard the high-pitched whine of a prop spun out of water, then the engine choking out, and then nothing at all 'cause we were soaring. We didn't teeter over the top. We didn't bump a bit into the air and slope down the other side. We fucking launched and we flew. At least five or six feet off the water, 'cause that alone was the height of the dam, and we sailed double that in distance. Flying in a boat is an odd and wonderful feeling. The adrenaline and precautionary painkiller spiked into my bloodstream had my brain processing lightning-quick; it slowed down time enough for me to appreciate the flight: calm and pleasant. And nothing like the landing. We banged down hard on a still, unforgiving creek that may never have had a single human grace its waters. We didn't glide our landing out, we just smacked and stuck. But hey, it worked. James's timing was perfect. The motor didn't come off its transom. The boat was not leaking. We were not dead at all. And so we slapped hands and yelled, turned up the music, popped the tops off our brews and toasted to our own glory. James wanted to shoot the dam for our return, but I didn't like the look of the slope on this side. Sometimes when you're up you should walk away. And so, foot to logs, we pulled the boat back over. It was agreed that we shouldn't tell Fred. Then we drove away, legends in our own minds.

LEARNING THE LAKES

THERE WERE TWO MIKES UP THERE, THE OTHER COMES later, this one is Fred's son. He was in his mid-twenties, thin, about five foot nine. I always saw Fred and Mike's smaller size as a disguise—they both punched well above their weight class, both big personalities.

I should comment on why I often describe guys in these stories by their weight. I didn't plan to; it just emerged while writing. I don't see size or muscles as what makes a good man. Not at all, not close. But when you're young, or at least when I was, it wasn't uncommon for disputes to be settled by being physical. That sounds dramatic but it's true. It starts early. Pulling another kid's toy away or holding on to your own. Pushing at the playground, monkey-bar fights, wrestling, even sports. Sometimes too you get in actual scraps. And I'm not necessarily saying that's a bad thing, when you're young. We've been humans for a couple hundred thousand years, evolving from some variety of primate much longer, but we've had third-party conflict resolution like laws and police and courts for a relatively short time. The impulse to solve disputes physically is in our makeup, our mind-set. We're working with paleolithic software here. It seems most adults grow out of it or learn to control it for obvious and good reasons. But when I was young and there was always the chance of an altercation turning physical, it just made sense to size the world up in relation to myself.

Anyways, Mike had a bunch of admirable qualities. He did some time for stupidity of his youth. He was all energy, smoked, had a series of tattoos including barbed wire with blood drops, the Tasmanian Devil, and the Nike Swoosh. We were good buddies, worked well together, fished in the evenings, drank sometimes, and shared a log cabin where we built a screened-in porch, then felled all the trees in front so we could look out at the lake in the evenings.

In my first week of my first season, a couple guides took me out to show me around the lakes. As we cruised in one boat, Mike was in another: a tuned-up twenty-five-horsepower two-stroke Mercury on a featherweight aluminum hull. This was effectively a type of rocket. He was cutting back and forth all-out across our wake. Back and forth, back and forth, shit-eating grin for his speed. On one of these passes, I watched his boat catch the angle of the wake and kick sharply, launching him high into the air, then down onto the water. The outboard motor jarred to a side, and the boat turned back in his direction.

Mike dove down under it. Unmanned, it then settled into fast, erratic circles in the middle of the lake. We motored over to treading-water Mike, saw that he was still alive, laughed at him first, and then helped him into our boat. With the chop on the water from his circling boat we couldn't saddle up and hit the kill switch. So with all of us loaded in the one, we left the other and headed for home. Mike and I dropped the crew at the dock, and then went back out. Sitting in the hull with a couple blankets under the stars, we waited for the runaway to run out of gas and got to know each other.

Up there and in those times nobody had GPS; you learned the lakes from people showing you around, and then tried to remember where lay all the many submerged reefs that mined them. As a result, some of us would hit them often—I pinged more than my fair share. On two separate occasions, I watched Mike and Les cruise along and as they shouted towards my boat where to meet for shore-lunch, their hulls bounced and their motors flew up, the prop spinning in the air, as they made their mark on submerged Canadian bedrock.

When I was still learning the waters, I followed Mike in my boat out to Simeon Lake, an hour away. Directing me with big arm movements, he made it clear that you had to steer a dramatic "S" turn in this small lake to avoid all the reefs in the middle. I followed him, laid those turns, and would do so for years. One day in a later season, another guide said laughing, "Just drive straight, there's no reefs there." Credit to Mike for a punchline lasting years.

NIGHT OF THE BEAR

EARLY EVENING ON A SUMMER NIGHT AND I WAS walking up to the lodge for a snack. A strange bird called. And then again. It came from the path under pines not far away. I was like the donkey who might starve, stuck between two equal bales of hay: *Investigate this peculiar bird, or keep walking for the kitchen?* That time of night I was at full leisure and wasn't in a hurry to decide. I decided to pee into the bushes. Finished, I zipped, it sang, and so I walked towards it. Turns out it was Fred making that whistle. And he's got a rifle. He was at the base of a big tree with Nemo, a black mutt I've never met another smarter.

"What are you up to?" I asked.

"That's the bear that keeps tearing open the shore-lunch shed." Fred pointed upwards with the muzzle of the gun.

A couple times a summer, every summer, a bear just being a bear would come into camp for all the smells and couldn't be scared away. Sometimes you'd throw rocks or fire a warning shot. There were no game wardens or traps up there. Sometimes we were probably too quick on the draw.

So there's the big bear just being a bear in the tree: not snapping his jaws or growling, just watching us. Nemo, who treed him, diligently at Fred's feet, me just in front of those two, and all of us gazing upwards. Fred has to be careful because the first cabin housing several American guests is about fifty feet away. He puts the barrel on my shoulder to steady it as he angles upwards in the pine. Someone placing a loaded high-calibre rifle on your shoulder where your job is tripod is an odd feeling. For all his intelligence, and whatever mine, no one thought to plug my ears.

Trigger pull: BLAAM. The gun went off beside my head like someone shot a gun beside my head. I was a bit stunned; the bear was worse. It fell fifteen feet down to the hard sand path. Nemo snapped his jaws at it, and the wounded bear lumbers away. Fred couldn't fire again at ground level because we were bordered by float planes, guest cabins, and drums of fuel. The huffing and grunting bear heads around the front of the lunch shed. Nemo's on his tail. Fred's following. In the dusk light I saw an axe leaning against the side of the shed. I grabbed it and went around the opposite side. As I came to the end of the shed, the bear lumbers out in front of me. It sees me but then turns to snap at Nemo. So right then I full swing hard as I can blunt side down. It thudded home heavy and the bear collapsed on the packed sand.

"Should I hit 'im again?!"

"Yeah!"

I swing and miss and sparks fly off the boulder next to the still bear in the semi-darkness. I swing it once more to be sure, and for sure, it was over.

Nobody else came down to check out the gunshot and all the barking, and maybe that makes sense. Fred started and backed up the Yanmar tractor. We struggled to lift and pull the dead weight of a dead bear into the trailer, but we got it there. With me standing on the hitch, Fred at the wheel, Nemo alongside, we drove in the dark, into the forest.

I went out a few days later to see the bones but the wolves had dragged the bear away. Other than a claw that I still have, I didn't find more than fur.

I helped kill a wounded bear shot defenceless in a tree. There's no pride to it. But I was eighteen years old and it happened. And it was night while we rode on the trac-tor—too dark to tell if I was smiling on that drive with Fred out to the woods.

SHORE-LUNCH MEMORIES

FOR MANY GUESTS, THE RITUAL OF SHORE-LUNCH WAS A draw as big as the fishing itself. It was a welcomed time to stretch your legs on the Canadian shore, its bedrock and evergreens, after the morning in a small boat. The guests relaxed with beers, the guides went about the work.

Seasoned wood was split, and a fire made. The walleye caught that morning were filleted, battered and breaded, while the fire heated canola oil in cast iron pans. Midday in the Ontario summer is hot, and we'd sweat cooking over the fire, arm hairs long singed off, and spin the walleye that floated and bubbled and browned in the hot oil where they cooked without soaking, spin and turn and flip them effortlessly in the short minutes they fry. We'd lift the fillets with long spatulas, hold them a second over the pan to drip dry, then lay the browned fish on paper towel and tinfoil next to pans of fries and cans of corn and beans for the guests to serve themselves first.

Some days after cooking I'd swim in the lake to cool down, float on my back, a soundless world from ears submerged, and look up at the big cloudless sky. If the breeze was blowing my way I might smell the lunch we just cooked—and I'd choose it today if it was my last meal. Or maybe I'd smell wood smoke and pine trees. Or maybe there'd only be the smell of fresh and clean lake water around me because it just wasn't windy all that often up there. If you went to that spot today it'd look the same. It's too remote to bring loggers. There's no miners. Some trees would have died and others regrown and it'd look unchanged. There'd be eagles. Wolves around but you wouldn't see them. Moose in the shallow creek beds eating pond weeds and grasses in the early morning and you'd see them if you were first to the area. There'd be moss on the rocks and fish in the lakes. You could go there now and it'd be the same. I'd get out of the water and climb onto the shore and dry in the midday sun before walking over and taking a piece of the still hot, still crisp fish to put on white Wonder Bread—not the brown molasses bread made daily from leftover Red River Cereal for ham-and-cheese sandwiches you'd take if you were portaging to Musclow Lake, with its own memories—but white Wonder Bread almost meltingly soft, butter sun-warmed. Slice and lay down thick raw onion, salt and pepper, a cold Coke. That's for me.

If your boat caught a hundred fish before shore-lunch, nobody besides you and your guests really cared, but if you showed up empty-handed, as could occasionally happen, there was a little shame in the other boats providing for you. Morale a bit low for those fishermen coming to shore looking to the other stringers to see if there'd be enough walleye to share, or if we'd actually eat all the beans and corn for the first time. If it was another White Boy coming empty-handed, I'd make sure to bust his balls. And if it was one of the Natives, I'd pretend I didn't notice, or tell him how we barely got ours.

If you were new and green to fishing up in those lakes, that made the risk of getting skunked even greater, but if you asked Jimmy Young where the fish were, he'd tell you if he knew. Jimmy Young was the oldest guide there and looked somewhere between seventy and ninety. He could have been younger though. His thin body had a curve to it that made his head sit forward like a turtle. And he did everything slowly, also like a turtle. Like some of the other guides, he had to make sure he took his insulin shot every day. Of the ten thousand people that have said *Hello* to me in my life, Jimmy's was the best. He kinda sung the word every single time, and he was old enough that it worked. He pitched high on the *o* then hung to it with a sound made through teeth gone missing like the buildings in North End, Winnipeg, *Winterpeg*, where he spent his winters.

On one particular shore-lunch we were four boats, eight guests, four guides. Cooking alongside me and Jimmy that day was Ira Henderson and Isaac Abraham. Ira Henderson was one of two Iras that worked at Sabourin, and they were nothing alike. Ira Henderson was physically well-built and had calculating eyes that squinted and beaded through you. Ira Henderson that mostly kept his own company, that spread rumours and spread rumours about me, that had done time, that always seemed a lurking menace. I never had any major conflicts with him and that was probably because I kept my distance. Isaac Abraham was a kind old guy who at that point had his sharper days behind him, sometimes forgetting where to show up for lunch, sometimes forgetting supplies. Like most of the other shore-lunch spots, that one was set up with an old forty-five-gallon drum cut in two lengthwise: one half laid on the rock as a stove, the other half at the next spot. You'd fill it with wood, get a fire going, and place the cast iron pans, kept in your boat, on top. In the space under the rolled sides of the drum stove we'd keep our fries warm in steel bread tins covered with tinfoil.

At this spot the wood was a bit wet, and the fire wasn't heating the oil properly. If the fish lie for long in oil that isn't just below smoking point, they come out soggy. Isaac poured on some diesel. Diesel doesn't blow up like gas. It helped some but mostly just coated and blackened the logs, fuming up thick curling smoke. He kept on with liberal dousing. After we had finished cooking, we were all eating, Ira Henderson sitting off by himself as he sometimes did, and we could still faintly smell the fuel. We had eaten most of our lunch before the first diesel burp arrived and someone pointed out that the fries had sopped up the excess that had splashed over the sides of the stove. You just couldn't tell while you were eating. We were all of us sick in the boats that afternoon.

Another day, Johnny Moore and I had cooked for our guests, and so we relaxed in the shade after eating. Johnny Moore was smooth. His name even sounds smooth. *Johnny Moore.* His boat was organized, his cabin clean. He could play the guitar, sing, was friendly with guests and they liked him. He was about fifty and still something of a ladies' man.

We were sitting there full and content and warm and looking at the water when Johnny rests his perfect smile, takes out his dentures, and brushes them with a small bush of needles from a pine branch. Johnny tells me with a voice all gums, "You should get a good Native girl. They're loyal. She'd fight for you if you got in a fight. Yeahhh," he said, "she would."

"That's cool," I said.

When I was first learning to guide, Johnny Moore taught me to skin potatoes. He said, "Don't be perfect, be fast."

How much of our present is our past entitled? How different are we from who we once were and how much does the passage of time erode? Maybe you see a friend you haven't in a long time and they expect you to be the same person they once knew. After seven years all the cells in our bodies have been replaced except a few in our eyes. I'm not the same young boy I was. In some ways I'm different than who I was only a few years back. What if we did something we regret? What things can be atoned for and what are beyond redemption? What do you hold against a person? What if Ira told me the nature of Johnny Moore's jail time but many years had passed and Ira spread rumours anyways?

Some windless afternoons with the hot sun overhead, a belly full of fried fish and fries and homemade cookies paired with the hum of the motor made for heavy, heavy eyelids. You'd fight it hard while driving: rest one eye winking and then switch. Or halfway close both. Or you close them both, but promise just for one second and count that second in your head and then open up. There were stories from before I arrived of guides falling asleep and driving up onshore.

We were on Mary's Lake after lunch and cruising at full speed when we passed smooth rocks bleached bone white a few feet from our boat. An isolated little pinnacle with deep water around it. I watched my two guests look at each other and smile knowing that their guide had such command of the waters: skirting dangers, threading needles, this *pro-show*. Meanwhile, behind them with my hand on the throttle, half-conscious winking away, I only just glimpsed that death-rock as it passed close enough to drag my hand over it. I sat up wide-eyed now and alert realizing where in God's name I was on the lake at that moment, happy we were not sent airborne.

Sometimes after shore-lunch a guest would want to see one of the trapper cabins that were spread out over the area. So we'd cruise out to one nearby and then idle in slowly, watching for deadheads so as not to ding the prop (I still managed to ding five my first year). The cabin would have been abandoned for the summer, and the land it sat on strewn with rusting conibear and leg traps, mounds of bones and skulls and teeth. It was eerie enough in the summer, it was something else to imagine the trapper living for months in the seclusion of the winter forest: its isolation, silence, and coldness. That man unspeaking and surrounded by dead things. The snow around him red with blood.

SNAKES

ONCE, I CAME DOWN TO THE DOCKS WHERE IRA ASSIN was cleaning his boat, and I said, "Hey, Ira, where's Josh?"

And Ira said, "Ohh, probably suckin' cock for fishin' spots."

Josh was the original White Boy up there, the first before I arrived. He and Ira Assin were the two best northern pike guides and nobody else was close. One time as I was walking past the guide shacks, I saw Josh do an impression. He stomped loudly with one foot while dragging the other behind him. I stopped walking and watched. Up and down the wooden deck walkway, stomping and dragging. I don't think he would have done it in front of me, knowing I was watching. His performance got some good laughs from Paul "Shoot the Little Rabbit" Fox.

That reminds me of this very short story from another place and I'll be quick 'cause it's a very short story and barely worth telling: Lana was about five years younger than me, so about six at that time to my eleven. She did me some kind of large injustice while playing in the sun on the grass with the other neighbourhood kids on a care-free Manitoban Saturday. Of course, I have no idea what that was now. Lana was tiny, blonde, a voice like a cartoon mouse, and the muscular dystrophy had her walking with her stomach stuck out and wobbling from side to side. Because of whatever enraged me, I let her know, I made it very clear to her that I could walk right and she could not. I looked her in her eyes, and didn't yell, just calmly told her, "At least I can walk right." She went home.

From a mixture of guilt, and fear because he found out everything, I walked silently beside my dad while he rototilled the mud perimeter of our house next to the crime scene. Shortly after, I marched my sore ass down the street and apologized to Lana's mom—Lana didn't come to the door. I'm sure her mom thought I was the Devil, or at least a snake, and if we are what we do, then that would have been a hard case to defend.

DON'T TELL FRED

AS A GROUP OF PEOPLE WITH HARD LIVES, I SUSPECTED Michael Keeper's one of the hardest. He was short, thick, a hard worker, surly, generally a bit nasty, and probably had very good reasons why. He was about forty but looked double that. He had wild hair, tiny eyes, a pockmarked scarred and broken-up face from a life fighting and drinking and falling asleep outside in the winter. The English some of those guys spoke wasn't great, and Mike's was the most broken. I can say all that now without offending him—never meaning any in the first place—because he's dead. Over those six summers, I did see him smile and laugh here and there, and it was something of a privilege, like some birdwatcher finding an uncommon thing, if you saw it.

You only needed about four fish per boat at shore-lunch, but Mike always showed up with a dozen, who knows why. That meant that much more filleting, battering, frying, and wasted fish. Then he'd undercook them, and if the guests asked him to brown them up a bit more, he'd just ignore them. He just liked greasy fish that tasted soggy, I think. Then they'd ask you to brown them up a bit more, and now you're in the classic space between rock and hard thing. I'd usually just say, "Can't do it." Mike didn't take well to my attempts at rational dialectic and compromise. Like I'd try to engage him in good ol' Socratic dialogue, and on more than one occasion his response would be to set his wrists upturned and knuckles down in this old Irish boxing stance, bouncing on the spot. He really did bounce on the spot. It was funny to see, but you definitely wouldn't laugh at him when he did that. He'd be one of the last guys you'd want to get in a scrap with. Probably a seasoned fighter, and the way he carried himself, I might think a dirty one.

One day when there were no guests to take fishing, he and I were working onshore together. We were clearing a section of trees. We felled a tree, then chained it behind the Yanmar tractor. I drove and Mike stood behind me on the hitch. While being pulled, the end of a log unearthed something in the dirt. I throttled down, put it in neutral, set the brake, and we went to look. It was an unlabelled old brown bottle about half full. A drunken guide could have stashed it a few years back, and then forgotten about it, like an old dog who's lost his bone. Or maybe a trapper dropped it who knows when. Mike seized it from my hands. His eyes widened. His gnarled and cratered face with a big red nose lit as much as its past would allow. "Don't tell Fred. Don't tell Fred. Don't tell Fred."

Okay, Mike.

LABATT BLUES

AT THE END OF THE DAY, THE LITTLE STORE BEHIND THE lodge, the only place you could spend money up there, opened for an hour or two. It sold some fishing gear and chocolate bars and other conveniences, but most guides came just for their beers, of which we were allowed two Labatt Blues a day. When you have a staff of eighteen-year-old boys and grown men with lifelong addictions, prudently, you restrict the flow of Labatt Blues. We flew in Beaver-load upon Beaver-load, their only cargo dozens of stacked cases of Labatt Blues. When the guests, all of them wealthy, wanted beers for afternoon fishing, or in the evening for dinner, that was their only option. For staff they cost two dollars a bottle, and you put them on your tab and squared up at the end of the season. Not everyone got their daily beers, but most did. And some, not everyone, but some that didn't want theirs would still buy them, and then sell to those that did, with a one hundred percent markup. A few of the older guides, the Natives, would appreciate the extra beers if you sold, but respect you more if you didn't.

Douglas Big George, that being his full and real name, was six foot seven, in his forties, and a long-time serving guide. He was not a bad guy when sober, though occasionally a bit of a dick. When shore-lunch was over, one boat had to take out the garbage bag of greasy tinfoil, tin cans of beans and corn with pieces of food stuck on them: a smelly bag of trash to be sorted for recycling back at the docks. If you were in the same party for a few days, it would only make sense to take turns. DBG would always say to me, "Garbage in the garbage boat," and throw that hot bag of shit in mine. Makes me laugh now.

When the guiding season was over in September, Doug would head back to Winnipeg and go on employment insurance, like most of the other guides did, like I did one year, and that would see him through most of the winter. He drank hard in the winter and was a dumb and mean drunk and served out a homicide charge because of that.

One afternoon I came down to the docks where he, smiling, put up his fists to me.

Ahh, play spar, friendly game. And so I smiled with hands raised too.

Doug said, "Hit me."

I said, "Nah."

He said, "Okay, my turn. You gotta give him one of these." He then leveraged that full frame to drive a knee straight to my crotch. I dropped to the sand and felt pain, that old hollow nut-trauma pain that takes you back to a playground somewhere. Turns out he was waiting at the docks for the plane's arrival to take him out on a mid-season break and had started the celebrations early. From where I lay curled up in the sand, I admired the sun's glint off the glass of some empty Labatt Blues.

HEAVY BOOTS

IN THE SPRING THE SHORELINE AROUND SABOURIN Lake had ice with patches of snow on it, but the middle was open and that's where Greg would land the Beaver. Fred, Susan, their big black mutt, Nemo, along with a couple of others and I, had already been there for a week opening up the camp, getting it ready for the other staff and guests that would soon arrive for the season. Greg would be the chief pilot that year, his first at Sabourin. But if you're flying a Beaver, you already have several years of bush plane experience.

It's hardest to land a float plane when the lake is glass because you have no depth perception; you can't tell if the water is just below your floats or still several feet off. And the lack of a headwind means it also takes longer for the friction of the water alone to bleed off your ground speed. Many more bush pilots are killed landing on calm water than rough.

Greg set the yellow plane on its loud approach over the trees and above our heads, smoothly closed the air gap between pontoons and the mirrored surface of the water, and set her down like butter. He turned and taxied the plane towards us, feathered the sputtering engine as he got close, then shut it down and silently coasted the final distance to merge pontoons against the tires of the dock. *Beauty.* Swinging open the cockpit door and stepping down to the floats in heavy boots, Greg was six foot one, close to two hundred pounds, tight white shirt tucked into jeans, crew cut. He looked like he checked all the military boxes except service. Twenty-six years old—that's young now, but not when I was eighteen.

It always felt special to be up at the camp first before the lodge and all the cabins swelled with crew and guests, before all the boats were taken down from their winter cribs, to see how the place had fared the harsh Northern Canadian winter with its heavy snows and minus-forty-degree weather. That evening after the small crew of us had all eaten dinner together, I went to my cabin, made a fire in the potbelly stove, and sat warm next to it in my bare feet, sweatpants, and T-shirt.

The sun was close to setting and it was cool out. Nemo started barking outside my cabin. He wasn't a young dog and wasn't easily excited, but bears and wolves were common enough and he'd bark at them. I'd gotten used to seeing bears regularly and up close, and so I wasn't persuaded to leave the warmth of my cabin. I kept reading.

Nemo kept barking. Flipping a coin without the toss, I decided, *What the heck, I'll have a look.* I opened the door and looked at Nemo. "I don't see a bear." He sounded off some more, then stopped. And then I heard it. Faintly. "Help." Just, "Help," over and over. It was far away and coming from the lake, which I couldn't see much of. I sprinted all-out barefoot over the hard sand path down the hill to the docks, a half-kilometre away. From there I could see someone way out on the lake bobbing and crying for help. Normally I'd have my pick from twenty boats ready to go, but at this time of the year whoever went out took the only one. Just back from the shore was a heavy, wide canoe with a square stern made to take a small motor. I'd heard it leaked and had never seen it used. "Hang on!" I dragged it into the lake, ran it out to my knees, jumped in, kneeled down in the fibreglass hull, and paddled as hard as I could. I was madly pulling strokes and already there was a small pool of water in the hull. "Hang on, I'm almost there." I was not almost there, but now I could see that it was Greg and he was up to his ears, and between gasps he was swallowing lake water. The combination of the lake's freezing temperature, his heavy boots, and however much time he'd been swimming before Nemo even started barking had him just about sinking. I yelled that I could almost touch him, that he made it — and that time I was closer to the truth. I got there and Greg grabbed the gunwale. "Greg buddy hang on you made it." I realized there was no way to pull him in given his soaking weight and this shitty vessel. So now I had to paddle back with him holding onto the side; the canoe, heavy and slow with water, still leaking. I couldn't believe he could hang on with his frozen hands, but he was a strong guy. "Hang on buddy we'll get there." The closest shore wasn't where I launched, it was a little ways down the shoreline and farther from the lodge. That's what we shot for, and I plowed the boat slowly ahead. I laid it all out paddling, straining everything I had every pull. I half expected him to let go, and wasn't sure what I'd do then. But behind me, coughing away, he clung. We continued on. And then Greg's boots graced pebbles under the water. And then he could stand. He waded haggardly onto shore, collapsed on the boulders, and kept saying how warm they felt, that he wanted to stay wrapped around one. I climbed out of that shit-canoe and left it in the shallow water. With his arm over my shoulder and around my neck, we scrambled straight in from shore to the woods, passing pine marten trap frames nailed to trees, and headed for the vacant trapper's cabin ahead of us. Greg and I, one unit, bombed through the door of the empty cabin and he fell for the bed. I packed that potbelly with dry wood and diesel-soaked sawdust from a pail in the corner. Lit it up. That little stove started sucking in air through the wide-open vent sounding like a train with its fast-woofing rhythm.

Greg was pale and listless and spitting up lake water; he was hypothermic and I knew that was a serious thing but didn't know what to do. When the stove's thin walls glowed red, I left him. "I'll be right back with Fred." Bare feet to the path and sweatpants soaking, I ran the distance back to the lodge in the now dark.

I burst through the door to Fred and Susan's cabin. (It's funny the sensibilities of a Canadian—I felt guilty intruding through their closed door like that but knocking politely with Greg down the hill seemed equally improper.) While panting, I told them what happened and the state of Greg. Fred got on the three-wheeler, me in the little trailer behind thinking he was going way too fast down the hill and that we were going to spill. At this point I was also wondering if I burnt that cabin and Greg down. We got there quickly and Greg looked no better than I left him. Fred and I pulled off his soaked clothes, then massaged the leg and back muscles so he didn't cramp up, to keep the blood flowing. Eventually Greg started to shiver.

We brought him up to the hill and Susan made him hot chocolate while he rested in his own bed. I was in his cabin just before he went to sleep: he was shaken up but all right. He thanked me.

The next day Greg told us he was cruising back from fishing, accidentally dropped a lighter to the hull, and reached down to grab it. His grip on the tiller loosened and the motor kicked sharp one way, shot him the other. No life jacket. We found the boat on the far side of the lake against the shore, undamaged.

A week later I was eating dinner and Greg, saying nothing, put down beside me a leather sheath. I pulled out the knife by its handle whereon was engraved my name. Nemo got a steak.

I don't know all the details, but I think you could say Greg recovered. He wasn't physically impaired and he flew the plane well. I'm not sure how it affected him mentally. Fred would later tell me that Greg said it rattled him. And how maybe the people you're supposed to be thinking about at that moment weren't the people you were thinking about. But I don't know all the details.

Camp had started to fill up and the last of the guides, the kitchen staff, and the waitresses were arriving. Janet's trip started out from the East Coast near Halifax, where she and Greg were from. Her last leg would depart Selkirk, Manitoba, heading to the bush, Ontario. To a lodge of fisherman and old guides and late-teenaged boys and fish and work and isolation, Janet arrived through the open plane door smiling. Twenty-four years old with long reddish-brown hair. And smiling, with long reddish-brown hair. Her smile. The wind had already started flirting with her hair. Janet.

Throughout the season all the guides and other crew ate dinner together except for the waitresses, as that time of the evening had them serving the American guests on the other side of the lodge. One evening the staff were eating dinner, and Janet came out from the kitchen and asked Greg something from a distance. Nobody was really paying attention, but the broad dinner conversations at that particular moment just happened to be subdued, so when Greg responded a bit dismissively, it seemed to me to magnify an otherwise minor humiliation. I recall that was not an isolated incident as the season rolled on.

It was another dinner and I was bringing my dirty dishes to the bin in the kitchen. Janet had both hands full with plates to be carried out to the guests. She saw me. She called me over quick, asked if I would scratch the tip of her nose, "'Cause it's itchy and I can't reach and it's killing me." She wiggled her nose around gratefully while I helped her in her time of need.

Some of the dinners for the staff were repetitive, and after a few nights of a meat main course, Janet, a fish-and-vegetables girl, was picking at her side dishes of potatoes and peas. I went out in my boat and caught her a single walleye, cooked it up on the shore below, and brought her her dinner. From that point on, Janet and I would spend more time together; she and Greg did not.

One evening I was with Janet in her cabin. Greg was outside of the cabin, not knowing me there, and was saying nice things to her. Thoughtful things. He was trying. I didn't feel all that badly.

Another evening came and again I was in Janet's cabin. And, again, I was sitting beside a warm potbelly stove in my sweatpants, bare feet, and T-shirt. Janet was reading on the bed. From outside the door, "Hi," said Greg. He knocked, but didn't wait for permission. The wood door swung on its hinges, and Greg looked like the first time I saw him: militaresque, big frame, heavy boots. He fixed on me and looked pissed off. I'd be pissed off. I was pretty sure I was going to take a beating. He charged me where I sat, tackled me. It was a blur and a scramble, he was swinging hard and landing. Sheer luck had the top of my head pointed towards his heavy fist in the tangle, it was bloodied up a bit but if it was my face it would have been pulpy. I don't think I got any shots in. Janet jumped on his back. (What do you think about that, Johnny Moore?) She was yelling, "Greg no! Greg stop!" while trying to pull him off. Eventually he gave it up. We were up and standing, the three of us, all breathing heavily exchanging glances. Nobody said anything, then Greg left the cabin.

I put shoes on and followed him outside and said, "Rush me when I'm sitting on the ground? Let's go." That was not so smart; Greg would have absolutely destroyed me—but heat of the moment and a girl and all. Thankfully, he didn't oblige.

That night Fred talked it over with both of us, but there wasn't much to say. I mentioned how he was treating her. Fred nodded. Regretfully, and in dramatic fashion, that same evening while Greg was in the lodge, I walked up to where he was sitting, and without saying anything, I laid the knife he gave me on the table in front of him. And then I walked away.

"Sorry. It's not personal," Fred told me the next morning. "He said he won't stay on if you're here." Greg was the chief pilot. I was a blossoming fishing guide and shore-hand. I was expendable. I went and packed my bags and the Cessna 206 flew me out that day mid-season. But everything and everyone gets forgiven at Sabourin and I would be back.

THE GAP

ALL BUSH PLANES ARE GRACEFUL IN THE AIR AND ALL of them are not everywhere else: water, land, ice. A float plane lands and lifts off elegantly, but once on the lake their turns are wide, slow, at the constraint of the winds, and there is no reverse.

There were two big docks at Sabourin. The left-hand dock looked like an inverted "L" or lower case "r" with the long side pointed out to the lake. The other dock, the right-hand dock, was its mirror opposite except raised several feet higher. The short end-section of each of the docks pointed at one another and a gap of about twelve feet spanned between them. At the end of the fishing day, the boats would drive through that gap to their slips and safe harbour for the night.

One day, the right-hand dock had an empty Beaver plane tied to the end of the long side. Now taxiing in on the water, another plane was coming to unload guests. Fred, Jordan, Susan, a couple others, and I were at the short end of the left-hand dock—the logical spot to park that incoming plane, which would keep it a safe distance from the Beaver. The Cessna approached, the sound of its propeller whipping through lake spray from strong winds. The trick to docking a float plane is to set your line as you get close, then cut the power and time the momentum of your coast on the water, accounting for wind. Come in too heavy and it'll be hard for the awaiting crew to stop your plane, you might bash up the dock or a pontoon, too light and you'll stop well short and someone will have to throw you a rope—safe but kinda embarrassing for bush pilots (I would later be a bush pilot so I can speak to their egos). As this pilot was trying to feather the throttle towards us, his engine quit and he couldn't restart it. The line he picked brought him tight to the other plane on the other dock, and the strong winds were blowing him backwards towards it. Soon they would bang up together and that could mean thousands of dollars in repairs and grounded flights. We listened to the groan of an engine being cranked but not firing up. This was a slow-motion train wreck and we spectated the distance between the two planes vanishing. Fred grimaced, his hands on his head, and gave something like an, "AhhgNo." There was not near enough time to run down the dock that we stood on, run over the shore, and run up the other dock to intercept that Cessna being blown backwards towards the Beaver.

Occasionally, just for fun, a couple of the White Boys would sprint the short end of the higher dock (the dock that had the Beaver tied to it that day), commit full speed to the jump, and land on the lower dock (where we now stood watching helplessly). The reason we did it was because if you pulled it off you didn't break your leg, and if you messed it up, you'd break your leg. Nobody had tried jumping the gap from low to high.

Now the planes were almost touching. *At least I'd have the wind with me.* I ran back a dozen steps, a couple bounces in place to prime my legs and visualize my footing, then I sprinted all I had, arms pumping past the others, and threw myself off the end of the low dock, into the air, into the gap.

I did not make it. But I almost made it. I clung to the end of the wooden and wet high-side dock and scrambled up it: a bumped leg, wet shoes. The pilot was on the pontoon of his plane and outstretched a rope to me on the dock: too short, it wouldn't reach me. But the wing of the plane overhung the dock where I stood and so I got behind the strut and pushed hard against it. The plane body was too big of a sail in the strong winds and I couldn't move it forward, I could only slow its path. It was slowly walking my angled body backwards over the dock. Head down, eyes closed, pushing. *Not enough.* Any second I'll hear metal on metal. And then a sound: *Bang.*

More exactly a loud *stomp*. Jordan, a spry and springy boy, had cleared the gap and planted his feet home hard on the dock planks in front of me. Now together pushing on the strut, we moved that plane forward against the wind, pulled it in, and tied it off.

THE QUESTION

FISHING FOR SEVERAL DAYS WITH THE SAME GUESTS makes for a lot of conversation time, especially on the days the fish weren't biting. Over the span of six years at Sabourin, one off the coast of Haida Gwaii, and one hunt-guiding in Northern BC, I asked all of those hundreds of guests this same question: *If you could spend a day in a boat with three people, living or dead, no language barriers, who are they?*

Some answered quickly. Some would reflect for a couple days and tell me before they flew out. Not many said philosophers; I heard Socrates or Aristotle only a few times. Some said old girlfriends with about the same frequency. More frequent than that, Hitler, so he could be pushed out of the boat. Jesus more than Hitler. Muhammad Ali was mentioned several times. A former or current American president was the second most common answer and reflected the demographic that could pay for a fly-in fine-dining trip. But there was a response with an order of magnitude greater than any other. A clear runaway.

"My dad."

BOOK TWO

BOYHOOD AND ONWARDS

A KID'S FISHING STORY

As a kid I'd walk down the end of my street to the Red River's murky water and mud banks. Stories of sturgeon so big, men hooked up horses to pull them out, Ray told me. I still believe it. The Red River started way down in the States, crossed the border, flowed by us north of Winnipeg, churned through the power-generating locks of Lockport with its record-sized catfish, and then much farther north spilled out into Hudson Bay. We pushed milk crates across its ice learning to skate when we barely knew how to walk. We laid miles of tracks on it with Ski-Doos after school. The Red River that sounded off cannon fire in the springtime when its thick ice cracked into slabs and soon after, once again, I could fish.

I'd sit on the bare slats of the dock our dad built, spit sunflower shells onto the water, and watch them drift away with the quick flow of the current. I'd sit and wait. One time I sat so still for so long a little bird landed on my pole and we both paid compliment of quietly watching the other, admiring our respective plumages.

I was raised to believe that a red-and-white devil spoon was the only lure you ever needed, and I stuck to my dad's guns for many fishless years. But inevitably, the son rebels. And with weight, hook, and a piece of shrimp or sometimes hot dog, I would cast my line out and let it sink to the bottom. You could tie on a bobber if you wanted to, or to the end of your toe just to say you did. Sometimes my older brother, Gord, or a friend came. Sometimes Mom and Dad would walk down and check in on me. Usually it was just me.

I walked down one prairie evening after my dinner while my parents watched *Jeopardy!* and *CTV News*, passing houses of both friends and enemies, of homes with dogs I could trust and those I couldn't. I cast my line, and my bait sank to the bottom of the river, waiting for a catfish to sniff it out. I wedged my rod upright between the dock and a nailed-on car tire. "Sturdy," says I to myself. And satisfied, I went to sneak some strawberries from Mr. Babaluk's Strawberry Farm.

When I came back, sticky-fingered and red-faced, my rod and reel that I had saved a season's worth of cutting grass to buy, haggled for between two different sales booths at the Mid-Canada Boat Show until neither would undercut the other anymore and both were very tired of me, *was gone.* Jaw dropped and seeded teeth: "Aw, man."

I quickly suspected my foremost neighbourhood enemy, who was nowhere in sight. I'd later recruit my brother to help me exact revenge on him in case he did it, and if he didn't do it, as a preventative measure to keep him from doing something like that in the future. I also thought there was a chance a big fish pulled it in—a story only a kid would tell himself. The river gave nothing away, its visibility measured in inches. I ran up the road and the hill at Kimberly Place to our home, grabbed another rod, weight, and hook, then ran back down. I cast and I dragged the bottom. Over and over. Nothing. But then while reeling in one cast, my rod bent. "I got something." It could be a sunken stick, but there was definitely weight to it. I kept reeling. Whatever it was was coming up out of the murk. And then it broke the water's surface and I saw it. I started bouncing on the spot because I was reeling in my lost rod. When I could reach out far enough to put a hand on its cork, I grabbed it and shook off the river's mud that fell down to the water in clumps. Then I reeled in and landed the biggest carp I had ever seen. His body golden, boy.

A BOY WITH A STONE

THE CONVOY OF THREE TENT TRAILERS PULLED BEHIND three minivans arrived at the campground and were unhitched at three neighbouring spots. The roofs were cranked up high; the wings for beds slid out.

Growing up, our three families camped together a lot, and this time we didn't go to White Lake or Birds Hill Park, we left Manitoba south for the States. The campgrounds were nice, and apart from being told not to speak at the border, I couldn't tell we weren't in Canada anymore.

After a duration that seemed approaching forever, our dads finally dropped our bikes from their racks, and my friend, Darren, and I got on them. At nine years old, he was a couple years my junior. We set out to explore the grounds for oak roots to turn into ramps, or for other kids to play with or plot against.

We were gone awhile but then got hungry, and so came back to look for imported egg salad with iceberg lettuce on buns. Everyone must have been out walking or napping because there was nobody at our campsite except a red squirrel.

Perhaps if I had had a bun in my hand, I would have tossed it a crumb. But I didn't have a bun. As a boy, I was always aware of what objects in my proximity were the right size to be thrown. Down beside my bare and dirty feet were several such stones. Naturally, I picked one up. The squirrel sat upright on its hind legs, its paws holding human food close to its frantic, nibbling mouth and filling cheeks. A big eye—it might have even had lashes like in the cartoons. It wasn't tame, but it certainly wasn't classically wild either. If you can believe me, there wasn't so much malicious intent here and I didn't put all my efforts or all my strength into the throw. But throw I did. And of course, I hit it and square to its body. I was surprised, though, this was all too easy.

So, Darren and I walk over and look down. Part of me thought that if that little red squirrel had been most gracious it would have either run off to die or passed to the other world bravely and quickly on the spot, its wits intact—it did neither of those things. A long time ago, God, in one of her rare, tender moments, made the animal kingdom's perhaps most cute and beloved species, and now one of them lay before us in a broken curl, spasming. It wheezed and shook. I felt very badly. It's either an idiot or just a kid that is surprised when the obvious consequence of something likely and intended happens. I was at least one of those things.

Well, with my back-asswards sense of virtue, I knew well enough that you don't leave an animal like that. And so I jumped my weight onto the squirrel to end the suffering I caused. Turns out I did that right next to the tent trailer of napping adults. I looked down at the body. I felt rotten. Darren's parents had woken to the sound of a little psycho outside their tent stomping out the life of a cute, pet-like creature. We heard them moving. And right then, my brother, Gord, appeared with a handful of bread. It turns out he had been feeding that little guy not long before we wandered in.

I made for my bike and got the hell out of there.

My relationship with Darren's parents seemed a little altered after that. Gord too was not happy and for the rest of that trip plus one entire month back home, whether we were walking down Kimberly Place with our matching backpacks for the school bus, or making our return walk home, or eating supper at the family table, or any other time we shared the same space, which was often, Gord did not speak a word to me. Who could blame him? That's a long time when you are brothers separated by only one year, but I got used to it. It became something of a new normal. I still liked him. I didn't hold it against him that he was holding something against me. Sometimes I'd hang out in his room and we wouldn't speak and that was all right too.

One evening at the supper table, Mom and Dad demanded to know what was going on. Why weren't we talking? Gord told them about the squirrel they already knew about. Now two brothers in tears at the kitchen table.

I told Gord the same thing my parents told me they had said to Darren's parents: A boy that didn't want the thing to suffer, after being a boy with a stone.

MY WORLD THE BACKYARD

I SAT IN THE DIRT IN THE GARDEN, A SMALL BOY. I MIGHT have been helping to dig up red potatoes or maybe I was just eating carrots that we'd pull from the rich soil then run them clean on the grass in long strokes until they shined and didn't look real. A small stone about the size of my little finger and the same colour as the soil in which it lay caught my eye. I picked it out, wiped its dirt on my pants. Its entire surface small grooves and the chipped-sharp edges so thin they were translucent, two tiny notches near its base for lashing to an arrow that would have rotted away centuries, maybe millennia ago. I was a small boy holding complete magic in his hand and sat there wondering who made it and who shot it and what it killed and if they were sad and looked for it when it was lost. I sat there speechless for a while. It's still capable of that.

Sometimes I got to watch the skilled hands of a WWII engineer teach me how to make bow'n'arrows from willow trees in the backyard. My grandad. Both he and his dad spent their summers in Northern Canada in geological research, the profession they shared. My dad, too, when he was younger, would be dropped off by float planes in the isolated North, surveying for resource companies. And I would go on to spend my summers in the Great North as well.

One day my dad came home from the dump where he had found a bow'n'arrows set with more power than the ones I could make from willow trees—Christmas in summertime. Occasionally Dad brought us treasures from the dump. I remember one time he brought Gord a partial socket-set or something we were surprised was thrown out. And he found for me the head of a pool-skimmer net. It had a hole in its mesh. We had no pool. I was quite happy and put it on the top of one of my forts as a type of radio tower. Gord and I had endless backyard games: the Don't-Touch-Ground, the many versions of tag, each subtly different and some imported from visiting cousins from the West, the classic ball sports. But there was one game that raised the stakes like none other. Where boys became ~~men~~ stupider boys. If nobody was home, we walked to the middle of the yard, pointed an arrow straight up dead centre to the sky, drew the bow back flexing its limbs as much as we could, and let loose an arrow—then we ran. This was skin in the game. The safest spot was under the treehouse, but we didn't always make that. Sometimes we'd trip in the excitement. There were times we felt the impact of an arrow thudding a bass note and burying its metal point deep into the ground next to us while the shaft vibrated its pent energy. Sometimes it took two sets of boys' hands to pull the arrow out from the ground. We only played a handful of times; we knew that if we got caught, the punishment would be severe: Dad would be very mad. We didn't want that bow taken back to the dump where the last dad had thrown it away.

Before my first rifle, before my BB and pellet guns, I had a Canadian Tire slingshot.

"Only in the backyard, only at a target."

"I promise."

By the next day I took it upon myself to expand my territory out to the mud perimeter of our yard. As I hunted for misshapen clumps of mud, a black speck appeared in the sky: its flight path directly overhead, I wouldn't even have to move—the gods clearly intertwining our fate. Okay, Lord, I thank you for this gift I am about to receive. Each pump of its wings closed our distance. Having looked over both shoulders and all around me, I picked a ball bearing from my pocket, loaded and pinched it secure in the leather patch, drew back to full draw. And with a shot none more pure, I sailed that steel ball straight to its chest. It thwacked home. *Thwack.* But the bird only rolled slightly, minorly annoyed, and kept on flying. From the corner of my eye I caught motion as the living room curtains fell back to their resting place. Two seconds later the front door opened. Each stride of his legs closed our distance. I thought of running but it would have been futile—the gods clearly intertwining our fate. He arrived and no words needed exchanging. Our prior agreement was fair so I couldn't fault him his law there; I gave no protest. In the open hand he presented, therein I put the slingshot. But what a shot.

For years during the winters as a kid in rural St. Andrews, I hung brass wire loops from tree branches. My junior high science teacher, Mr. Adolf Marchuk, sketched out for me how to set them just off the ground and strung to branches where below cottontail prints ran in the snow. After school and on weekends, I'd walk my little trap-line, sneaking along the borders of the neighbours' properties, looking for the grey fur bodies hung frozen in the night. Just like in the stories I read and reread from sweetly smelling pages of old hardcover books. Gifts I still have from uncles and grandfathers I don't.

I got off the bus from school one summer afternoon and walked down the street to the house where Dad was tilling the mud perimeter of the yard. He told me to pick the weeds out in front of him. I dropped my schoolbag on the grass and started pulling them up from their roots in the soil, tossing them to the lawn to be collected later. When the engine quit I looked up and he called me over.

Churning up the soil with the tiller he had unearthed something that now lay in front of us. He tore it free from its garbage bags and duct tape. Covered in grease, foreign writing scrawled on the receiver, and a metal stock that hinged out from its body was a gun like I'd seen in the movies. My dad drew on the full extent of his hunting and firearm knowledge and pulled the trigger as it lay on the dirt. What turned out to be a Russian engraved AK-47 automatic assault rifle, was unloaded. We took it into the garage and snapped pictures holding it in combat profile, because assault rifles have a lot of charm when you're ten. I tried to convince my dad we could drill out the trigger or cement the barrel and still keep it, but the police came as called and we handed it over.

LOSING GOD

I took the idea of God very seriously as a small boy. My parents were Christian and with bowed heads we blessed our supper at the kitchen table each night. But even that being the case they weren't very strict about religion and didn't force it on us. I simply took to the idea of a God and heaven and understood what that belief entailed. For several years I was the most devout in our family.

Growing up, we would drive the forty minutes from St. Andrews to Westminster United Church in Winnipeg on most Sundays and always on Christmas Eve. It was a big beautiful old stone building with tall stained-glass windows backlit by morning sun, and a large organ with golden pipes many times taller than I was. The choir was thirty voices strong and included my Grandma Lois. I don't recall her ever waving back to my pew, though. On Christmas Eve the lights would be turned off and their voices along with a hundred more from the congregation sang "Silent Night" to the melody of a solo violinist playing in candlelight. It was beautiful. You could feel it.

My brother and I shared a room for over a decade when we were small boys, until he moved out to his own room in the basement, and so I set up a cot on the floor next to him for a while. As early as I can remember, we ended our night by saying in the dark to each other: "Sweet dreams say your prayers." And a voice would reply from either a higher or lower bunk bed, "Okay you too." Every single night for years we did that with no other words added or missed. Nobody told us to say that. Funny kids.

My youngest conception of what God looked like was from the Canadian-produced TV show *Size Small*, which ran from 1982 to 1986, me being born in 1982. There was a character that had arms and legs attached to a massive music-record body. It had drawn-on eyes and a smile, both fixed in their place. It was just this big dancing smiling presence on the screen and it related to me some concept of the supernatural. I remember thinking that that was God. He cameoed on *Size Small*. I was very young.

Sometimes my parents and I would watch *X-Files*. I used to love that show but I didn't get to see the end of many episodes because one of the characters would inevitably use the Lord's name in vain. They would say "Goddamn" or "Oh my God" or some variety, and so, reluctantly, I would get up and leave the room without saying why. I just never thought it was worth compromising an eternity in heaven for breaking a commandment. The risk-reward on that was terrible and I recognized that from a young age.

Before I was big enough to man the walk-behind mower on my own I'd walk in the space between it and my dad, him behind me trying not to step on the heels of this strange boy in front of him. We'd pace back and forth across the lawn together. The yard was about an acre and the walk-behind mower cut a narrow, narrow swath each lap, which meant that by the time you finished the whole yard, the first pass you had made earlier was about ready to be cut again. The grass cutting rarely stopped at 19 Kimberly Place. Today if I smell fresh-cut grass I think of my dad. One day that will make me cry, but not today, 'cause the big man is still going strong. At about eleven or twelve I would cut some of the neighbours' yards for cash-money and one of them was part owner of the local golf course. At thirteen years old I applied to work there as an after-school and weekend job and Mr. Ewert said I could be a backshop boy, washing clubs and driving power carts. I saw only one problem: I'd have to work Sundays. There was a commandment against that.

After church the next Sunday I asked my minister for a sitdown. My parents waited patiently on a pew in the empty congregation not knowing the topic of the consultation. I explained to him my moral dilemma. He said he too had to work on Sundays. I thought that was a good point. He said as long as he had one day of the week to keep holy, to not work, that was reasonable. Essentially, God was cool with it. I appreciated how there was room for interpretation in the scriptures. I took the golf course job.

I should say I wasn't some sort of puritan kid because I took the idea of God and an afterlife seriously. On that spectrum I was closer to the opposite. I was a bit of a wild-child class-clown smart-ass and made things hard for some teachers and parents and other kids. I'm sure some of them remember me. It wasn't uncommon for me to be kicked out of class and sent into the hallway for lots of little dumb pranks and jokes. My ass was rarely not mooning someone. I got in the odd fight and skipped the odd class. But all the while I still operated under the idea that I had a personal relationship with God. You see stuff like that even in adults. They'll do all kinds of egregious acts but think to themselves that God is on their side, in their corner, knows they're special. Meanwhile that same God is letting thousands of other people die every day from preventable causes, curable diseases, famine, unclean water. Some seventy-five million people died in a few years in the Second World War but God is looking out for me, helped me win a Grammy or a boxing match or saved me from bankruptcy.

Religion for me was never where I got my sense of right and wrong. I thought the commandment forbidding work on Sundays was sorta arbitrary; I didn't get the rationale underlying those ethics. But I wanted to uphold it because I believed in God and wanted heaven. It was more like the game Simon Says. Why would anyone that believed in heaven take a chance of losing out on it? Some ninety-odd earthly years of obedience for an eternity of pleasure. There's not much to think about, and I told myself that when Mulder or Scully were being irreverent. But those weren't values, that was just a weird kid's cost-benefit analysis. Values I got from the people around me: family, friends, and culture like TV and movies and music. I don't lie now and don't think I ever really did as a kid either. I might try to change the subject or divert the question or dance around the truth but when my parents were wise to my shenanigans and questioned me directly about what I was up to, I routinely confessed and suffered the punishment. I'm not saying that to build my ego or as a testament to my character, because I've failed myself and people in other ways, it's just not from lying. Nor is it from stealing: one time I was with a buddy and we were in the high-school store at lunch hour. Sometimes friends of mine would five-finger-discount candy bars. I never had before but I thought I'd try it this time. My belief in God wasn't wavering then, I just got better at rationalizing the odd time I strayed. I'd tell myself it's just kids being kids rather than an unforgivable transgression that would cost me everlasting life. Like God would spot me the odd sin because he knew overall I was a good guy. When the cashier wasn't looking, I grabbed a Pizza Pop and put it in the pocket of my hoody. I walked out and told one of my buddies and we ate it. But I just didn't like that feeling, it wasn't what I valued, and I didn't do it again. On the last day of school before summer holidays I brought an envelope from home, put the exact change including tax for the price of a Pizza Pop inside it, and folded in an anonymous note explaining how I had stolen one a while back. The school store was closed outside of lunch hours so that's when I slid it under the door. I didn't repay that debt out of a fear of God.

I wouldn't be surprised if I never missed a day of prayers starting from an age too young for me to now remember. I said them in my head so there was never an issue about looking peculiar at a sleepover. Then one evening up at Sabourin I was talking to Fred and the topic of God came up. He said he didn't believe. That was the first time in my life I had met someone that said they didn't believe in God. I just never met a self-confessed atheist or agnostic prior to that. He rattled off some reasons like how random the world's events are, evolution, bad things happening to good people. And this was coming from a kind, intelligent, honest, family man. That evening was the first time I entertained the idea of there simply not being a God. The second night after that conversation was the last time I ever prayed. I was seventeen. I wasn't sad about it nor did I feel lost without it. And that's surprising to me because you'd think a person would feel a little down about losing eternity.

Half a dozen years later I guided off the coast of Haida Gwaii and one day a former priest was my guest. He had preached to a congregation for a lot of his life but he lost his belief so he left the faith. Of course I asked what happened. He said that a truly powerful and loving god, one that could square a circle, a god that could make a stone too heavy for itself to lift and yet lift it and also not lift it, would not allow for a world where bad things happened to good people. He said the concept of free will does not justify evil because a truly powerful god could permit free choice while also not allowing harm to the innocent. Someone could throw a stone at a child, the child would feel no pain, there'd be no injury, and for the thrower of the stone there'd be no guilt or punishment or even sadness of not being able to cause someone else pain—*all the while, there still being free will.* The first time I heard that argument it took me a while to wrap my head around it. Its parts don't make sense because they're mutually exclusive—but a true god is not subservient to logic and could make 2 + 2 = 5. I don't see a way around that argument. I think it's tight. It's the same one I kindly bring up to the proselytizers that come to my door every year. The last time that happened was about six months ago. After hearing the two priests out, I explained that dilemma. The older one couldn't understand what I was saying no matter how many different ways I tried to deliver it. The younger one did, and he said he would think about it and get back to me. As I type these words today, I'm still waiting.

DYANA

THE NIGHT HAD COME: *MY FIRST SCHOOL DANCE.* I STOOD near a wall holding juice or something. We all did. And then I heard it: *Boyz II Men.* I knew that was the one. Under the basketball hoop, the disco ball turned slowly, glittering like I knew her world was. And, "Dyana, would you have this dance with me?" *My first slow dance.* There may have been daylight between us, but in my mind I was living the lyrics of those smooth Black men. I lead you through a series of grand, tight shuffles: hands wet on your waist, hair wet on my face, shirt wet on my skin—everything wet. Shifting my weight from foot to foot, movement like a sea buoy, to our tender, predict-able fate. You never once had to guess where our next step would take us, love. I spun you slowly, without spinning, in a square. *Dyana.* We never danced again. *We didn't need to.* Did Michelangelo repaint the Sistine? But you broke my heart when so quickly you moved to the next boy. And then the next boy. And the next boy.

BACK TO THE BUS

WHEN HE WAS SIXTEEN AND I WAS FIFTEEN, MY OLDER brother Gordo got his licence. Oh, sweet Lord. Now we're cruising—now we're in a fucking car, man! A 1982 red Volvo. She and I were made the same year. If you like squares stacked on rectangles, this fine Swedish piece of ass was geometrically perfect. We had the mix-tape engineered well in advance: the build-up and joyous explosion of "Magic Carpet Ride," a bunch of forgotten stuff in the middle, and we'd timed pulling into the high-school parking lot with Less Than Jake's ska smash hit, "Johnny Quest." Mostly songs barely known, now forgotten, that never belonged together in the first place. Those were good days.

Not long after, I went to one of my first parties. I was stone sober but remember little. I think we played Twister. I do, however, remember wandering out from the basement party to talk to the cool-ass older brother, Chris, of the girl that hosted it. I poked my nose in his room stacked with CDs. I looked them over. One said Blink-182. I had never heard of it.

"I like this one," I said, "was gonna buy it soon." He lent it to me to get me out of his room. Awesome. Just awesome. This meant that I'd also have to return it to cool Chris. And in the meantime, I'd say things like, Yeah just borrowed this from Chris. Chris lent that to me; that one's Chris's. Yeah, Blink is Chris's—it's awesome.

And once again came another sweet Friday, Mom didn't need the car for work. I'd dubbed the Blink CD to a Volvo-compatible tape. *Let's ride.* Then Gord let me know while he was laying out Cinnamon Spread on his Kub bread, and I was hammering back Golden Grahams, that he'd be taking Garret and Rob and Joey in the Volvo that morning—*no room for Tommy.* It hit like a fast boat on shallow reef, like a knee to the groin during casual conversation: always doing their worst when expected the least. It would be back to the bus. The goddamn bus. Full of enemies, and smells, and inopportune boners. I was reeling inside and salty tears flowed into the bowl of sugary milk. Then Gord asked, "Hey, can I borrow Blink for the drive?" My internal hemorrhaging slowed as my quality musical taste was recognized.

"No, you can't. No, you can't." That helped a bit.

KADE

Two boys both alike in pride and size,
In fair Selkirk High where we lay our scene.
From recent grudge break to new mutiny,
Is now the two minutes traffic of our stage.
The fray:

First time they bumped into each other in the hallway they both looked back over a shoulder to see who it was and if it was intentional. Neither apologized and they kept walking. Could have been an accident, most likely was, but now there was tension.

A few days later in front of the cafeteria's glass windows, chance lined them up again. Neither altered course, neither gave way. *He won't move for me, so I'm not moving for him. Don't know anything about him, but fuck that guy,* thought both boys to themselves. Their shoulders hit again.

They both turned a head and exchanged glances, but walked on.

There was no dialling this back down—there was no reason to have dialled it up in the first place.

Later into the week, a midday lunch bell filled the hallways as kids left classes. This time they caught sight of one another from far off 'cause they were lookin' 'cause after the last one it was inevitable now. They kept walking towards each other. Neither boy softened his posture and they leaned into it to make it count, and again their shoulders hit, this time hard.

One boy turned around, raised his hands. "What's up!?"

"What's up with you!?"

The loud hallway got quiet quick; school fights were always electric.

They squared off and said a bunch of stupid things, swearing and macho dumbassery. Binders were thrown down. It was pretty quick, each getting some shots in. Later, one boy's acquaintance said, "You could hear it when you hit him." And that boy liked to know it. The fight was broken up by a teacher jumping in, grabbing them, pulling them apart and into the empty cosmetology classroom. And while waiting for the principal to come, the boys said things like, Shit man, you got me good, and, Yeah, you too, man. And they were cool with each other.

They were suspended for a couple days including the rest of that afternoon. One of the boy's moms came to the school to get him. She didn't seem too mad on that drive home from Selkirk to St. Andrews. When his dad got home he took it about the same, not mad mostly just concerned, knowing these things happen with boys. The dad asked, "So did you get him?" That particular boy had a few friends but maybe not the greatest, and that evening when his mom asked, "Why didn't any of your friends call?"

He said, "I don't know." And felt shame.

A few days later, classes had finished for the day, and that boy stood outside waiting for the bus. He was with a couple acquaintances. The best friend of the guy he fought was a big 'roided-up nutbar and approached the boy and got in his face and started swearing and calling him out while other kids watched. And his skinny weak little acquaintances—who can blame 'em—did as much as the other dead leaves on the ground their eyes rested on. This guy could destroy this particular boy and so he just stood there, just sorta takin' it, while people watched.

And then a friend of a friend of the boy slowly walked over. "Hey Tommy, how you doin'?" said Kade Panting. Kade Panting, same height but thick, an enforcer on Junior A. And fuckin' Kader looked that guy up and down slowly, didn't say one thing, just looked him up and down, then put cold unblinking eyes into his. And buddy right then looked down and walked away.

The very next day that 'roided guy apologized to that particular boy in the hallway, saying he didn't want anything to do with Kade, heard that him and his brother go at each other with bats, is what he said.

You're a fuckin' legend, Kade.

TO THE END OF THE WORLD

BETWEEN SEASONS WORKING IN THE NORTH, I WAS enrolled at the University of Manitoba taking philosophy and literature. I was walking between classes and I saw a student exchange program for Northern Brazil being advertised on a poster in a hallway. I knew nothing about Brazil, the Spanish language, or what I would even study there. The placement was not for a major city like Rio or São Paulo, but for a smaller city up north, and no students from our school had yet gone. I applied to the program, was accepted, and came up with the idea of studying Brazilian culture and literature and turns out—not Spanish. Half a year later, with a student visa, I flew to Rio.

The back story of Brazil before the love story of Argentina. In the first hostel I stayed at, I met two guys travelling in their late twenties. They surfed well and were good with girls, and so checked all my boxes in what I looked for in role models. They let me travel up the coast with them where they were headed by bus, the same direction as my school a thousand kilometres away. After a couple weeks of pulling into new and small coastal towns where often I was the only blonde young man, and the minor celebrity status that afforded me, I began to think I could have a very genuine cultural experience, many of them, without being enrolled in school.

Eventually, as we neared my destination, I split off from those guys and arrived by bus at night to João Pessoa. I didn't know where I would stay, I had no money because my bank card had stopped working in the last town, and I couldn't speak more than a few words of Portuguese. This was all a little distressing to me as I sat in the dark at the bus stop with my bag and the surfboard I had bought in the last town. In the nearly deserted bus station, a guy in a white muscle shirt wearing a gold chain said hello, in English, and asked if I needed a ride. My mind rang alarm bells—they warned me about situations just like this. But the thing is, I felt like I had no options. I decided to tell him about the school that was expecting me tomorrow, my cashless predicament, and then use that to feel him out, probe his intentions. He said, no problem, he'd take me to a hostel in town and that he was in medical school. He wasn't dressed like it. I straight up told him I know I'm not supposed to take this ride. He laughed and said he could understand my position. I gotta use the bathroom a second, I said, stalling.

I went there to think it over, hoped he wouldn't steal my surfboard. After mulling it over, I came out and he and the board were still there, so I took the ride. My palms were a bit sweaty in the car, but we talked the drive, he seemed like a good dude, and the hostel he dropped me at was very nice. He and I would be friends for my time in João Pessoa.

After about a week of trialling the school program in João Pessoa, and to the disappointment of the exchange coordinators who were nice people and had made efforts to have me there, I made the decision: no more pencils, no more books. That meant the next eight months were wide open: no destination, no travel guide, barely speaking the language, with no cell phones back then, and with a debit card that still didn't work forcing me to make in-person cash advances at banks with my Portuguese gibberish and then carry relatively large amounts of money on said person.

Even though I had quit school, I took to João Pessoa, made some friends there, and decided to stay awhile. One morning I sat with a coffee on a couch at the hostel. Johnny Cash's cover of "Hurt" came on TV. There was only one other person in the room and it was an older man who I suspected didn't speak English. Our lives can be seen as an unending series of coin flips: you say something or you do not, you stop to tie your shoelace or you do not, and all of these seemingly trivial and incessant details determine who we fall in love with and whether we get hit in traffic. We're flipping through a toss right now. Every moment is a missed opportunity or it's one made. In the seemingly mundane hides the profound. Another day I would not have said to the older man beside me, "What a sad last song at the end of his career." But I did, and Eric Schmidt, German, responded. He said he was from Doctors Without Borders and was in the process of moving in with his girlfriend and her daughters. He invited me to have dinner with them that night. I happily accepted. Later on, they would invite me to live with them, and so I did. All things arising, a future entirely changed, from that one little comment about a Johnny Cash song.

I found Eric to be good company and would sometimes join him for coffee in the city, in addition to dinners at his house. It was in an afternoon when we were walking that he clutched his arm, an ache in his chest. I took him to the nearby hospital where he stabilized then recovered quickly from that heart attack, and we left the hospital the same day.

My banking problems after I had fouled my Canadian debit card's PIN three times on the foreign keypad plagued my whole trip down there, and Eric said he would help me open a joint account, allowing me access to a Brazilian debit card and currency. He also told me how easy it was to buy gold on the black markets there, tip the border guard to overlook your baggage, and sell it in Germany on the public markets. He proposed we do that. It made some sense to me and I said I'd think on it. One day I received an email from the school I hadn't attended in weeks. It said this gentleman I was hanging out with was a suspect character and known by local authorities, and I should be careful. I don't know how they knew where I was keeping myself or who with. One day Eric failed to return to that house and his girlfriend and, despite my emails, I never heard from him again.

Nearly two months in Brazil had passed. I had made some day and overnight trips with friends to neighbouring towns, but I always returned to João Pessoa as my home base. My Portuguese was improving as most of my girlfriends spoke only it, but when the Brazilian police called me into their precinct after being informed by our two countries' exchange coordinators that I was no longer enrolled, thus making my student visa void, and told me I had two days to leave the country, the four of them and I still struggled with translation. Eventually, with the clarifying symbology of hand gestures and taking turns scribbling pictures on paper, we understood one another, I think. I tried to say something like, "No hard feelings, I'll remember your country fondly." But with the intensity of the moment and my aversion to Brazilian jails I could have jargoned out only God knows what nonsense, like, "No feelings give more pain, I will not forget this." Their stares were blank and their faces grave. I nodded and left.

I gave my surfboard and heavy Doc Martens leather boots I never once wore and have no idea why I brought them down there to a boy that lived with us. I found a bus that went west straight across the big country on a forty-hour trip leaving the next day and took it. And I never went back to Brazil with its nurse that asked me if I wanted more stitches and the gay doctor who hit on me while I lost blood. I never went back to your roses and cigarettes smoking on sidewalks in Macumba black magic, to your capoeira beaches and sugarcane Caipirinhas and all your beautiful people and food and music, but your memories are warm ones, Brazil.

The bus took me to Northeastern Argentina, a country very different from the one I had left. I liked Argentina a lot, and over the next several months I would see much of it while making my way south, also taking the occasional sojourn into neighbouring countries along the way.

While finishing a backpacking trip among big granite peaks and glaciers in the south of the continent, I was in Chilean territory when I ferried across the Strait of Magellan to Tierra del Fuego, the island Chile claimed half of, Argentina claiming the other. I hitchhiked all day on a straight and endless road with no cars. I still have a picture of that road. A person's day of walking never looked so predictable as that. A road with a few curves at least allows the imagination to conjure up people, vehicles, something around the next bend. This was not such a place for imagination. Finally, well into the afternoon, a truck approached, slowed, a window unrolled. It was the Carabineros, the Chilean police. They scolded me not to hitchhike, but then mixed the message by offering me a ride and a place to stay at their barracks that night in a bunkhouse. My feet were sore; I happily accepted. Those Carabineros were nice; we had pasta. The next day they drove me to the border where I walked across to Argentina and continued my way south. I hitch-hiked all the way down to Ushuaia which then was the world's southernmost city, and is still nicknamed today "The End of the World."

On both that island and back on the mainland, I'd hike and camp in the Andes Mountains and the foots of them. I bought a fly rod and cast it on rivers and lakes, but did not know what I was doing and ate canned spaghetti in the evenings. I near froze in the mornings with no sleeping pad under my sleeping bag—but all of it felt very romantic anyway and I knew I would tell someone about it one day.

One day I arrived at a campground fronted by a mountain lake and there was a man sitting by his camper next to my site. My Spanish was conversational at this point, and we talked and I asked him a lot of questions about fishing down there because he fished too. He invited me to dinner and I happily accepted, then left to make some casts.

Later, I'm walking back to the campsite with my hands not smelling of fish and I can see him at his picnic table. I can see him now too. He's preparing meat, salting it. The sun's setting behind us. There's a fire going. His wife walks in. And their daughter. She was Argentina. She was Argentina.

Moira had long black hair, was wearing a black tank top and a black-and-white skirt the length to her ankles. I pretended to barely notice her as she slid one finger then the rest under my ribcage, encircling with her open hand the thing she considered pulling out and throwing on the fire—or letting beat on. She smiled while she did it, and I looked away.

We all ate around the warmth of the fire, had wine. I talked some, listened mostly. Her dad gave me coca leaves to chew on and then ball up in the side of my cheek. The evening grew late, her parents went to bed, and Moira and I stayed up.

The next day we all got in their car and spent the warm hours lounging and swimming at another lake her dad drove us to. Soon, they would be going on to another campsite in another town and it was decided I would meet them there. It was both all of us and the two of us passing more days of hikes and swims, and campfire evenings of dinners, and nights.

Moira asked if I wanted to visit her farther north in La Plata, the provincial capital of Buenos Aires, where she lived with her sister and her sister's boyfriend. I did want that. We made plans to meet there in a week. We parted; I bused. The camp spots where I laid my tent now seemed entirely without charm after the time spent with her and her family. Those days passed slowly, but eventually I made Buenos Aires, then headed eastwards to her parts. For the next two months the four of us took turns making dinner every night. On weekends and late into the night we would go dance in clubs where it felt like everyone had the same vibe from excellent house music. Sundays were for relaxing, eating freshly made stuffed bread on the grass at the markets where at midday guitars and violins played folk music, where she taught me to dance traditional Chacareras to the sounds coming from under shade trees where others danced too. Weekdays we'd read at her apartment and on park benches and explore the city and go see movies.

Also, we were in love.

There exist different systems of time. There are clocks with longer spaces between seconds where more things fill their span. You dream a day's events in minutes. Your car skids to the cliff-edge and in a moment the sequence of your life plays out. Go fast, time ticks slowly; increase gravity and it does the same. Our time was unique and felt longer lived than the turn of two calendar pages.

One night I told Moira I had a surprise. We walked a few blocks away to the park and then up one of its narrow paths to a bench streetlamp lit under a blossoming tree. We sat there and she said that was nice and then we heard a dirt bike coming towards the location I had given earlier and it rode up and dropped us off a pizza with a little ribbon on it and she said that was nice. Then a young man I met on the street in Buenos Aires busking his violin and whom I had propositioned to head to La Plata that evening and had paid half up front and told him I'd pay the other half after he plays and yet whom I never asked to wear a suit walked up out of the night in the park and handed us the bottle of wine I had handed him earlier in the day and he played three songs for us in his suit before I gave him the envelope and then she cried and said she was coming to Canada and I said, good.

More days of dream things passed, but I had to go back home to the North, to Sabourin, to Canada for work. Moira started her visa applications and all the paperwork. She started making the bus trips to Buenos Aires to see it through the bureaucracy of her country. We talked on the phone and missed each other and said so. She told family and friends of our plans.

A few months later, while I was working back up north, I told her I wasn't ready for it. That was not an easy decision and I felt very badly. It felt like something worse than just hurting her feelings, and that was bad enough. It was like I dirtied a clean thing, some sort of wrongdoing to the innocent and what was innocent wasn't her alone. The love of life that took me to new places and led to me meeting Moira was the same drive that kept me leaving them. I was young. I said that I was very sorry. Sometimes you're the one causing that pain and sometimes you're at the receiving end. Both times there are never words enough.

She said, "But I've been doing all my paperwork."

THE RIGS: PART ONE

NOT ENTIRELY UNLIKE THE GOLD RUSH OF THE 1800S that brought men to the North seeking quick fortune, the oil and gas rigs that drilled the surface of the northern provinces offered anyone with a driver's licence willing to work in minus-thirty-degree weather before the wind chill a hundred thousand dollars in their first year, and promotions based on seniority, not merit. And so I spent a couple winters there.

When the price for oil and gas was high the drilling never stopped and our fourteen-man crew was split between day and night shifts. The boys on my rig had come from sea to shining sea: from BC in the West to the Newfies and their Haligonian cousins from the East, both speaking their charming accents. Our roster had a few suspect characters given the nature of the work and formal education not required, but there was a camaraderie built around getting the job done well on your shift as a team, and leaving it in a good place for the crew that changed you out twelve hours later.

The rig I worked on was more advanced than most that came before it and those in operation at that time. Many tasks that required manual labour on other rigs were either partially or fully mechanized on this one. That meant the work was easier on the body and accidents and injuries were reduced—not nil, but reduced. It was a fortunate time to start working on them.

One evening near the end of a shift, I was using the hydraulic lifts to roll a special type of drilling pipe, called *collars*, in their steel-frame crib to line them up for the big top-drive to screw into and send them down the hole. These collars were about twenty feet long and weighed four thousand pounds each. I was trying to save a step and instead of properly positioning myself in front of the controls, I was awkwardly crouched under the crib. I pulled the wrong lever and rolled those collars to the opposite of the intended direction. They fell four feet to the frozen ground next to me, thudded heavily with deep vibrations I felt up my legs and into my chest, and banged loudly on each other inches from my ankles. I easily could have had my body or leg where they impacted, and they would have made me very flat.

There are two general types of subterranean gas: *sweet* and *sour*. If the gas should upwell and expose itself to a human, one does not kill you, and one does. You have to make labelling clear when promotion is based on seniority, not merit, and here they really nailed it. *Sweet-Alive; Sour-Dead.* Usually the gas a rig is drilling for does not come to the surface. It's kept down in the hole, in its recess of the Earth, by the weight of the drilling pipes and a liquid mixture called *mud* that fills the hollow pipes and the hole itself. If that gas should come up unexpectedly, you're *taking a kick*. That's *bad*. If the pressure from that kick is too great and you can't hold it back with the weight of the mud and valves and air bags, it can blow things apart, send things high into the air, and potentially ignite. *Bad*. If it's sour, it can do all those things while poisoning you. *Very bad*.

One night shift, with no drilling connections to be made, I as a roughneck was walking an inspection round to check for anything out of place. Eventually, I ended up making my way to the space below the drilling floor to have a look at the *stack*: a ten-foot-high, four-foot-wide piece of equipment made of heavy steel components and valves. The rig's drilling pipe runs through its centre that sits on the surface above the deep hole being augured. Usually there is nothing very interesting to see at this area of the rig, but it's a critical area and worth a peek now and again.

When I opened the big doors that closed it off, I saw the extraordinary: mud from the depths of the hole was bursting up out of it, shooting with high pressure all around the stack, blasting into the bottom of the drilling floor like a volcano—*liquid mud everywhere.* I ran out of there, doubled up the stairs, and yelled it to Colin, our driller.

"Holy shit!" said Colin. He tore out of the drilling room, *the doghouse*, grabbed the railings of the stairs and sailed himself down the flight without touching any steps, turned the corner, saw it: "We're taking a kick!"

He turned around and doubled back up to the doghouse where he slapped the red alarm button. Lee, the rig manager onsite, a moose of a man whom we called *Dad*, ran out over the snow from his shack a short ways away. Dad gave us orders, we followed procedure, slowed the pumps, shut valves to hold back the gas, and the fountain of mud spray tapered off. With hard-lined gauges, we monitored the pressure of the trapped gas held back behind the valves and prepared to divert it.

The lowest-ranking crew position on the rig is a *leasehand*. If you were a derrickhand or a driller, or any other position, that's where you would have started. And that night he had the unenviable job of walking out to the flare tank, a ten-cubic-foot metal container with an open ceiling a hundred feet away, connected to the hole by piping. Once there, he would drop a flaming bucket of sawdust and diesel inside of it. *I promise.* Then when he had safely distanced himself, the valves would be opened: the gas vented and burned off.

And so Cory, the godforsaken leasehand from Alberta, with two front teeth missing from a hockey puck, and donning his safety glasses and hard hat, walked out in the snow in the dark with his flaming bucket. Name your price, if I could have a picture of that solemn figure in the night tiptoeing his vial of nitroglycerin to bore the railway, I would try to pay it. Godspeed, brother. In steel-shanked, steel-toed rubber Dunlops, Cory stepped a ginger foot, and then the next, one after the other over the crusted snow until he made the red walls. Having arrived, he climbed the flare tank's welded ladder, slowly lowered his burning payload, relaxed his grip sweating inside his Green King gloves wrapped around the pail's handle, climbed back down from the ladder to snow—and then he ran the fuck away.

Valves were opened and the controlled burn-off began. Either we got unlucky because we unexpectedly drilled into a pocket of shallow gas, or we got lucky because the volume was minimal and the gas sweet, the result was flames that barely licked above the red walls of the flare tank, and the gas quickly spent.

THE RIGS: PART TWO

GORD, MY OLDER AND ONLY BROTHER, STARTED WORK-
ing on the rigs before I did. He took a couple years off
about the same time I started, then returned to the company I had just finished with. When he left the rigs he
was a motorman: the position between roughneck and
derrickhand. But if you leave and return, once again you
have to start back from the bottom and work your way up.
The responsibilities of a leasehand are mostly cleaning,
errands, and odd jobs.

On a winter day shift in Alberta, Gord was cleaning
around a cooling fan of a large resting engine. Without
warning, the engine and its fan started up, pulled in his
rag, pulled in his hand, and took off four fingers. Gord
called me from the ambulance on the way to the hospital.
Incredibly, he could speak calmly, coherently, and that
was before medication or painkillers.

After we hung up, I called the company headquarters
to have them contact that rig, find the fingers, ice them,
with the hope that they could be reattached. From how
the fan had severed them, how it had taken them from

the knuckle, that would not be possible. Mom and Dad flew out to be there.

While at the hospital, a father, suffering through the wounds of his son, made a request to the surgeon that would be denied. A request made not from wanting to *be* loved, but as an act *from* love: from the pleasure of loving someone profoundly. This he would later tell me he would have been happy to do. He asked that they cut off the fingers from his own hand and stitch them onto that of his son. Tell me something greater.

TO THE COAST

ONE MARCH IN MY EARLY TWENTIES ON A BREAK between hitches on the rigs, I came down from north of Edmonton to Calgary and met Gord for the Mid-Canada Boat Show that was stopping in his city. We had food and beer and checked out the displays of boats and gear. I stopped at a few different booths marketing their sport-fishing operations. One of them was called *The Salmon Seeker*. For the summer season, guests would be flown in on a turbine Otter float plane to a bay on the mid–west coast of Haida Gwaii. I may always hear *the Charlottes* when people talk of that place, that's what they were called when I worked there, but I'll catch those words before I speak them and call them Haida Gwaii out of respect for its people. The guests would stay aboard the 150-foot ship, with fine dining in the evening, after a day of guided fishing on one of the smaller Boston Whaler boats. It was likely the very best salmon fishing operation in the world: there was none more remote; there was no fishing pressure in the area; and the chinook salmon, kings of their species, were still far from their spawning ground and full of fight having just returned from years of growing to size out in the wild Pacific. The two gentlemen at the booth listened to me pitch them on my years of lake guiding, that I was good with boats and people, that I would love to work for them if they would roll the dice on me. I got lucky, and with no ocean fishing experience, no ocean boating experience, knowing nothing of tides, having never seen a live salmon, they took me on crew and I jumped right into a guiding position for the season. Go figure.

There's a cult around confidence with some people. A worship of it. That to show hesitance or self-doubt is weak, less attractive. I never had a problem with trying new things and putting myself out there. When I was young, I'd sometimes feel anxious arriving in a new city by myself if I didn't know where I'd stay that night and didn't speak the language well, my heart pounding when the plane was landing or the bus made its final stop. But I'd put one foot in front of the next and try to stay composed and find good people. I was astounded how far a genuine smile took me, the language gaps it filled. It was like putting up a flag others could recognize. I didn't learn that on my own, someone told me to do it. I'd always been able to walk up to a pretty girl and say hi. I could camp in the mountains by myself and hike in the dark with meat on my back in bear and cougar country, fly bush planes to remote locations and land on small lakes. But everyone has things that challenge them. I used to love speaking in front of crowds up until about high school, and I don't even think there was a traumatic event that caused a change, but in the years afterwards that would be something that took effort. Still does. When something feels hard, *there lies growth*. I tell myself that. Sometimes I feel that I'm supposed to be good at something because I've done it in my past, and if that thing feels like a part of my identity and I don't do it all that well, it's a shot to my character and my confidence. But that's bullshit. Execution matters but so does effort. Nobody does everything well all the time. It's a boring little safe box of a world where a person only does what they know they can pull off. A bird's-eye view would show a lot of those small boxes, people alone inside afraid to touch the walls, and not knowing there's another person like them in a box close by. That safety itself is an illusion. I don't want to die regretting the shots not taken, and you get stronger even from missing. It's not confidence that wins the day. Values and courage and effort and willing to fail and fail in front of others and if they talk let them because those that talk don't matter so do it over and over again if that's what it takes because that's what's shiny in people. What's strong in them. If you don't push back on the walls, the box you're in gets smaller over the years. So push back. Push fucking back.

I went to Victoria on the West Coast in June where I met the guides and crew. We loaded the big ship with food and supplies, and then the on-board crane hoisted onto the decks of the stern and bow twelve Boston Whaler boats, fourteen feet in length, each with 150-horsepower motors and 9.9 kickers. We left harbour and sailed three days up the east side of Haida Gwaii, around their top, and back down the west on the open Pacific, en route to our destination, Kano Inlet, an isolated and uninhabited little bay sheltered from the big storm waves up there. Everything about this was new to me, and taking in the scenery for the first time of the steep banks of British Columbia mainland dropping to the sea beside it was majestic.

The longest-serving guide, Andy, and the head guide, Brett, would take turns training me, both incredulous, both utterly dumbstruck that management had sent up someone with no ocean experience; someone grabbing the steel downrigger cable by hand, and falling over in the boat from the gentle roll of the sea. But it's hard to undo that staffing decision when you're in the middle of nowhere with no replacement at hand—advantage, *me*. Twelve-hour days seven days a week of repetitive tasks meant I picked it all up quickly enough.

That whole season we had no days off, an all-male crew, and three guys per bathroom-sized bedroom, yet never had a single fight, hardly an argument. Maybe everyone was too tired from the long days and early mornings, but it went smoothly.

Before the first guests would be flown in, our crew of twenty was still setting up the ship, outfitting the boats, breaking in the equipment and new guides. It was three or four a.m. and I was lying asleep in my bunk, two others in theirs beside me. Other than the distant drone-hum of the ship's generator in the engine room, the ship was quiet and I was deep asleep. Out of silence came the entire opposite: a scream highest in pitch, top-of-the-lungs, some manner of death cry. Not a yell, *a scream*. Knowing there were no women on board, I couldn't believe this sound was from a man. There are times in your life you feel called to action, that you know in that moment it's up to you to prevent something terrible from happening: and right then, hearing that scream, I knew this was *not* one of them. *I did not move, I stayed right the hell where I was. Let this thing sort itself out. There are rooms closer to wherever this horror is going down with bigger dudes who have worked here for seasons—I'm not moving.* After a few more wails, it stopped. Wide-eyed and adrenaline-coursed, I lay for some time wondering how many fewer would be up for breakfast.

The next morning I cautiously looked around, looking into the faces of the crew eating at the table to see if their alarm equalled my own. *Who is not here?* It turned out our 250-pound Kiwi chef, Toby, was prone to the occasional night terror. Then, so was I, Toby.

Salmon fishing does not want for beauty: sharpening a hook to needle point, machined aluminum single-action reels metallically ticking out drag, the feel of cork gripped in your hands, the fresh sea-smells, twin rods bent over flat sunrise seas where below the herring cut-plug rolls forward with spiral motion at depth in the cold and dark ocean for big springs that when caught and risen shine radiantly silver and black and purple in the water beside the boat. The fight might be the best there is. The eating is excellent. One fish can yield twenty meals. If I were arm-twisted to acknowledge the trade-offs, they'd be the boat trolling your lure, the downrigger holding your rod, the flashers imparting drag on the fight, and the impurity of fighting a fish against the push of the motor. That's different than a line arced from a cast that sails a fly to a still pool. It's different than thumbing a baitcast spool to land a heavy lure between lily pads where the sound of it breaking the surface angers a big northern pike who then moves from where she lurks to erupt the water, absolutely erupt the water, and kill that thing out of spite. It's different than holding a rod in your hands and feeling the bite. But it's pretty great.

On other days, a different prey: We'd sit on anchor, the head of a salmon stuck on a circle hook weighted to the reef two hundred feet below, stubby rods angled out from the gunwale. You might sit there for an hour or two if the lolling of the boat on anchor in the waves didn't make your guests puke and chowder the water. Sometimes during the monotony of that calmness there'd be a subtle *tap . . . tap . . . tap* on one of the rods. Everybody's head turns. Everybody stares at that rod tip. *Tap . . . tap . . . tap* like first raindrops before a thunderstorm. And then it's all fury. The rod violently jerked bends in half, line rips out screaming drag. There's no finesse to this fight: sit, grab the rod, hold on. Have the drag set right. Take line when the fish allows. Keep that up, be smooth not jerky, and the barb pinched off when salmon fishing but legal now should do the rest.

I'd be standing beside my guest watching, coaching as he fought it raising it from the depths, until we got our first look. Upturned eyes, green body on top, big sucking mouth, wide tail. My fisherman would draw it in closer and try to sweep this barn door on a path beside the boat. And if then it relaxed for a second from its struggle, I'd get a chance to spear in a steel harpoon tip tethered with five feet of cable to an orange *scotsman* buoy.

That stab would ignite the fish's rage again, thrashing and ripping line back out, spinning the drag, sounding for the bottom with fin thrusts churning blood in the eddies. Little room to stretch against the violence, the fishing line could be snapped or the hook pulled from its mouth—but now it didn't matter: buoy and tether.

And then we'd wait. Wait quiet, long seconds, even minutes, while the fish fights a rigged battle against buoyancy. Wait until the scotsman bubbles up from below and breaks the surface. Then hand over hand, pull an anchor from where it lies two hundred feet below on the reef, idle the boat over to the bobbing orange float partially submerged under its load. Below and drifting like a red scarf caught in a picture of the wind, blood and strength empty to leave the big fish suspended and weak and green in the blue water, its last throbs of life pulsing before fading and out. And then the halibut is pulled into the boat. And if, somehow, it still has any life left, you take that from it.

I'd lash a rope around the thick tail then thread it through the gills and pull it tight to curve the fish up. Even lifeless it could still spasm, and a large halibut flexing its muscles can cause havoc in a small boat, knock someone down or into the water. We'd head back to the ship for pictures, then fillet and freeze. And back then I never felt much remorse for what could have been a big egg-laying female no longer producing.

In the half-light of dawn, dressed warmly, exhaust smoking on the black water, my guests and I with the rest of the fleet idled away from the ship in its bay. We throttled up and cruised northwards farther along the coast to fish new grounds. We arrived, dropped lines, and the salmon were biting there like everywhere else.

One of my guests was reeling in a chinook on an Islander reel the colour of the now-risen sun. The fish just a few feet from the boat, I had my gaff in hand and was ready to swing. "That's a keeper." Then I see a big dark mass directly below the salmon, rising. This was a freaky thing; whatever this was does not happen in Manitoba's waters. The enlarging object, now just below the fish, was coloured a pink and whitish hue at its centre. And then our salmon was lifted up and out of the water in the jaws of thousands of pounds of Steller sea lion. This creature turned away and dove with its prize, the reel unspooling, and reemerged a couple dozen feet out. A huge, bulbous head above the surface, long whiskers on a dog face: we stared at it, and it stared back big black saucer eyes on this amoral bastard. The fisherman pulled the line until it snapped from the unmoving sea lion. Then without breaking its stare, and slowly at first, it wagged its head at us. It shook it. This was gloating, pure and simple. Over and again, side to side in a victory wag, with the fish's tail flopping. Then that teasing head shake picked up to mean intentions, and the sea lion ripped that big live salmon apart sending blood and guts into the air, into the water. I watched jaw dropped.

The first time it happened this was something spectacular to behold, but after the scene kept being repeated, it was just annoying and made it hard to get our limit. They saw us as dishing them up easy meals. And so we let the lions have their waters. Though less frequent, cruising killer whales would occasionally poach a salmon from our lines too, but always at depth, never the surface—they never meant it as personally.

On the crew of *The Salmon Seeker* was a general-hand and cleaner named Jimmy, from Victoria. He might have been a bit sore that he, with more ocean fishing experience, was not guiding and a prairie kid was. But he held his grudge more towards management than me and we got along.

If two people disagree and neither can win the other to their side, but the dispute has an answer, I like putting something on the line rather than just arguing. Like poker, it's not the gambling, it's backing up a conviction, filling up empty words. My dad, brother, and I often did this when I was growing up, even now too. It seems it's in my blood. One time with the leisure of a Christmas Day in rural St. Andrews, my dad and I were talking about tires of a vehicle freezing to the ground. I have no idea how this conversation started but outside of the living room window we could see the Eddie Bauer–edition Ford truck on the frosted driveway. My dad held the intellectual position that the truck would be frozen to the pavement and could not be moved under the power of a man. I disagreed. We each rationalized our point trying to convince the other how totally clueless he was. We invoked our layman's understanding of the physics and chemistry involved but with the conviction of men much more learned on the subjects. After some time of having made no progress, a case of beer was put on the line. I recruited my brother, which my dad allowed under the conditions of the wager. The three of us went outside to settle it, while Mom, and my sister, Pam, watched from the living room window.

Gord and I got behind the truck and planted our Sorels firmly on the pavement. We tilted our toques back so their pompoms wouldn't be in our way. We breathed up. We looked into each other's eyes with the bond unique to brothers trying to best their dad at something stupid. Then we leaned all we had into it and damn near blew our gaskets under the strain because the truck did not budge. Dad thoroughly enjoyed spectating our failure. Then Gord walked out from around the truck and opened up the driver door and put the vehicle in neutral. We returned to our positions. And then we easily pushed it a foot forward. We slapped high-fives and decided on foreign beer in the luxury of the moment. The bet concluded, we left the truck in its new resting spot just ahead of four bald patches on the pavement and went back to the house to listen to Rita MacNeil's *Christmas* and Anne Murray's *Christmas* and Kenny Rogers's and Dolly Parton's *Christmas*. Anyways, Jimmy, too, was inclined to wager on things.

It was the night of Joel's birthday and when we were done cutting fish and eating dinner, we were all drinking, and by the time this wager came up we were all hammered. On a balcony near the top of the ship about thirty feet off the water, we could see the stern where earlier we pushed off the filleted carcasses of halibut and salmon and watched in those waters dozens, *dozens,* of sharks up to five feet long, probably just dogfish but sharks nonetheless, feed on and fight over and rip apart those carcasses. But there was nothing to see in those waters now because it was night.

Someone asks someone, "How much to jump into the water from up here?"

I said, "A hundred dollars."

"Booked." Jimmy calls me out or thinks the entertainment value alone is worth that price.

So I stripped down and I was thinking, *The cold water won't matter for the seconds I'll be in. Those big fish will be scared by the noise. I've cliff-jumped that height into lakes. I like taking money off Jimmy. Easy game.* I jumped and sailed and splashed and swam triumphantly back to the side of the ship. Jimmy was out a hundred bucks, and I was up it. It took me a second to realize my vision was impaired from more than just the booze. A cocksure naked man had flown through the air bespectacled, came up de-spectacled. Net loss: three hundred dollars.

There wasn't much to do on that ship when we weren't fishing. The day would start around five-thirty a.m., we'd get on the boats not long after, return to the ship around five p.m. to cut, pack, and freeze the catch. After dinner, you might tie up some leaders for the herring cut-plugs to be trolled the next day, or clean your boat. Then mostly we just watched movies, read, hung out, relaxed. There were some weights and bars for working out.

It was Doug's birthday and early in the night and we were only a couple drinks in. The rain was falling pretty hard and some of us were out at the stern of the ship under an open-sided shelter that housed the vacuum packers. Work was done. A bottle of rye was being passed around. People were talking, laughing. You could hear the rain falling.

Dave did a chin-up on the shelter frame above us. Jimmy said, "Darren could do the most." Darren was about twenty, 140 and wiry. A cleaner and general-hand, nice guy.

I said, "I'll put a hundred against that." And we hand-shook it official.

Jimmy was glowing because, "Oh shit Darren's been doin' chin-ups every day for weeks yeah boyyy getting m'money back," and went and grabbed him from inside the ship. T-shirt, sweatpants, sneakers, Darren walked under the shelter. Rain was falling. A bottle of rye was being passed around. He jumped up to the bar and they're counted off. All the way down, then all the way up is one. He's quick for a dozen. Slows for a few more. Squeezes out his last grimacing for eighteen. *Eighteen is huge.*

Jimmy's jacked and talking smack, "Oh shit, my boy Darren payday!"

Of all the exercises: lifts, curls, squats, presses, whatever, I hate chin-ups the most, so I always thought that meant they were working. I'd also been doing them every evening since we sailed. I'm a little embarrassed about how keen this memory is for me: I can be under that tent if I want to.

I took off my hoodie, emptied pockets, dropped any weight, wiped my hands dry on my pants—my heart pounding. Eyes were on me. I jumped for the bar and sent up my first. I got to ten and Jimmy called out nine. I got to fifteen and Jimmy said fourteen and I laughed halfway up correcting him. It was a couple words as I passed sixteen. A few shouts at seventeen. I can hear them when I hung at the bottom for eighteen. It was a group of good guys under the rain in high spirits. Maybe my ego, a silly contest—but not all of it. Something mattered to me. Still does. It's not admiration, nor pride nor glory nor victory nor vanity. It's not respect. I can hear the rain falling outside. A bottle of rye is being passed around. People are talking, laughing.

TO THE MOUNTAINS

I FOLLOWED A GIRL TO OXFORD, ENGLAND AND TOOK any job I could find. I liked the girl, didn't like the office work, and after several months, *that was enough of that.* I made the obvious next move: embellish my resume and mass-email it to hunting lodges back home in Canada. One outfitter agreed to take me on so there I headed.

Up in the far north of float plane-access-only BC and a week into July training and scouting, I levelled with my employer that my hunting experience was more limited than I made it out to be. But I was eager to learn, could hike all day, and after seven years of fish guiding, I was good with customers. It's hard to undo that staffing decision when you're in the middle of nowhere with no replacement at hand—advantage, *me.* Bryan had a good sense of humour and let me stay on. I'd learn to hunt for Rocky Mountain billy goat, Stone sheep ram, grizzly bear boar, and bull moose. This was big mountainous country where you'd be dropped off to remote lakes with your food and supplies on your back for a week. Where you'd glass far away over vast alpine open spaces, hike the distance, and camp at a new spot every night. I'd see big caribou fast-trotting over treeless expanses; waist-high timber wolves from all-black to all-white hunting along ridgelines; an unprovoked wide-racked bull moose charging and fatally goring a cow moose forty feet in front of us; a wolverine scrambling across a shale basin that echoed its crossing below us.

In September and across a valley on a mountainside blushed red from late-season blueberry bushes, we glassed over a dozen grizzly bears while they grazed. Today that hunt is banned, but on that trip the American hunter paid over twenty grand for the opportunity, bought a licence where part of the fees fund the sustainable management of wildlife and their habitat, and employed several guides, equipment retailers, pilots, and cooks along the way. I was a packer on his five-day hunt where we were dropped off by a Beaver with our food and small tents. On day three, he made a clean shot on a mature boar. Our packs heavy on our backs, several kilometres into our return hike out while still up at alpine, another large grizzly fixed on us with lowered head and beaded-up eyes. The hump of muscle above its big shoulders rolled with each step. Each step, this closer bear. The few trees up that high were stunted, and without taking his eyes off Bryan, the bear climbed over and flattened a pine tree in a display of dominance. Less than fifty feet now. Fire a warning shot and then if he charges you're trying to gun down a running six-hundred-pound mean ball of thick hide, muscle, claws, and teeth with violent intentions. You could try bear spray but I'll let you go first. There just wasn't much we could do so we packed him out as well.

I was over two months into the season and on my third solo-guided hunt for billy goat, "the beast the colour of winter." Mountain goat is the most challenging of the Canadian big game hunted animals. They aren't hard to spot, like sheep can be, but they live in the nastiest terrain, the highest and with its weather. Then if you do find one and can climb to it and figure you can pack it out, you have to decipher billy from nanny. It can be hard to tell, and many nannies are unintentionally harvested and that's harder on the species.

My hunter was a man in his forties from the Mideast US. The float plane dropped us off at a small lake and no spot I guided was prettier. You could see the glacier's ice fields that fed down into the blue lake while you stood next to it, snow-sided mountains surrounding and close.

There was a canvas wall tent as base camp—so that's cots and a wood stove, welcomed for a late-season hunt. That evening we cooked steaks and mushrooms and onions on the flat of the little stove. I picked over my hunter's gear looking for dead weight: cut the toothbrush in half; a quarter roll of toilet paper rather than full;

dehydrated meals. It all counts added up. Five days of food, one tent, two rifles split between our packs that looked good and balanced for the morning.

We rose early in the dark and started hiking around the lake to the far side where we would make our attempt through the trees for alpine. The glacier's wide creek bed that would span a hundred feet in the spring was only a couple feet across now, and we followed its rocky and pebbled ground before we scrambled up its bank. Somewhere in there morning light peeked over mountain tops. Even without climbing we could see the lower parts of the mountain that potentially held goats: a basin, or the snow patches surrounding bluffs above the fringe border of subalpine trees. We sat on our dropped packs, pulled on toques, and glassed for the dirty-white hue yellowed from soil and piss: a billy goat's coat.

Two months ago when I arrived up there, I helped pack for the head guide and his guest on a sheep hunt as my first trip. Six days we covered ground up high and scanned non-stop without seeing a single Stone ram. It wasn't until the morning of day seven that Chad picked out horns on a camouflaged body in a grey rocky basin five hundred yards away, called it a legal curl, and was right. That's exceptionally good guiding. But sometimes you get lucky because we hadn't even had lunch on day one when I said, "Goats."

"Where?"

I pointed a hand without lowering bino's.

"Got them. Four?"

"Yup. No way to tell if they're nannies or billies from here." We still had a hike ahead of us, but now it was game on. The decision: "Do we drop our camp gear and extra food to be light on our feet?" That would mean we'd have to hope that they're billies, then climb, stalk, retrieve, skin, pack out in a day. I made the call. "Let's do it. We can always head back up there tomorrow if we like it but don't get one." He agreed. We dumped excess gear to the middle of the dry creek bed that I waypointed. We took one last look at those big snowy beasts. We entered the trees.

The two of us, guide and hunter, picked our way through the timber at the start of the mountain's lower incline. Climbing farther, my hunter started labouring in conversation, and after stopping for water, we went silent and higher.

On other hunts, I sometimes ran into cliffs or sheer walls, steep shale slides or devil's club—all kinds of a mountain's barriers. But today we gained steadily. Midday had passed now, and gradually the trees became sparse and shrank in size to stunted firs and pines. Our binoculars detailed the rocky outcrops emerging ahead of us as we went looking for our cud-chewing friends that should be close.

In whisper, "There." I pointed.

"Got 'em." Two goats in the snow on the next spine over.

"Probably the same ones we saw. The others likely not far off." I got out my spotting scope, mount it on its tripod, zoom max to 40×. I shed my glove, and my fingers in the cold air dial the horns into focus: their length and curvature, their bases where I'm hoping to see big thick glands. Like I said, it's tricky to differentiate. But sometimes you just get lucky and you know exactly what you're looking at because he turns away from you and lets you spy his big dangly white furry balls.

"Balls," I said.

"Nice."

"Range?"

"Three-thirty to the lower billy," said the hunter.

The mountain's spine we were on dropped down gradually beside us and in the direction of the goats. If we tried to get closer we'd lose sight of the animals in the process, couldn't be sure where we'd pop up, couldn't be sure they wouldn't move. You like to get as close as you can, but in mountain hunting, four hundred yards is not an uncommon distance from which to pull the trigger.

"All right. You like it? Feel good about it? You said you're comfortable out to 350." I said that as insurance. I'd brought him within his shooting range to a legal billy. That was the objective. I was still new to guiding and it felt good to have done that. Now it was on him to make good.

"Nice-looking animal. Yeah, 330. Okay." He says that without entirely selling me on his conviction.

The two billies stood on a flatter section of the spine, and anything below them was blocked by the treetops coming out of the gully between us. Goats are tough, thick hide like armour, and sometimes they can take a few shots to keep them down. We both chambered a round into our rifles, but mine was just for backup. No wind, calm cold clear mountain day. With our backpacks for shooting rests and our bodies laid out prone behind them, we each cast an eye through rifle scope glass.

"Okay, man. Take your time. Get steady. Calm your breath. We got time."

"I'm shooting," he said.

I plugged my near-most ear.

His rifle cracked loud.

The goat dropped without a step from where it had stood in the snow. It started a slow slide downwards, and then out of view, hidden by the trees. The other goat bolted away over the ridge and out of sight.

"Beauty. Nice shot, man!" It was. "He didn't tumble away fast, I don't think he went far, should be fine." I stretched an arm and slapped the back beside me. "Okay, watch that area in case he gets up and climbs back into view while I pack up my bag. When I'm done we'll switch."

I zipped and strapped, feeling good about the hunt.

"He's back in sight! Should I shoot?"

"Yeah, drop him!"

His rifle cracked loud.

We both watched the animal fold to the snow and slide down out of sight again. "Man, good shooting. All right, you pack, I'll watch," I said. And the hunter zipped and strapped.

"Shit, it's up same goat same horns same path! Should I shoot?" I asked because I never want to shoot for the hunter. But his gun was strapped to his pack now and we didn't want a wounded animal getting away.

"Yeah, do it."

I held the crosshairs high up its back for the distance and squeezed slow until the shot surprised me.

My rifle cracked loud too and 30–06 heavy-grained lead headed goatwards.

"Got him. Down again."

"Incredible. Tough bastard."

"Yeah, no kidding." We watched awhile. No movement. "Let's go."

We hiked down off our spine, into the trees, and up towards the next one. It took some winding of trial-and-error paths, some light rock climbing. We got there.

"Wow," he said.

"Oh shit." Thickly furred, beautiful long white coats. *Coats.* Two of them. Two identical billy goats with the same horn length, both males, these twins. "Damn. My fault." I felt badly. There was nothing good about that.

You could label it inexperience, but I bet even seasoned guides would have thought it the same goat and shot.

And our workload was now doubled: skin two goats and I'm not very good at that, pack up the hides and horns, pack up the meat, hike it all out. And it was already well into the afternoon in the mountains where we didn't know the weather.

We had some food and water and took pictures. Then, knives out, we skinned the hides, sawed the head from the spine, cut the meat off the bones, loaded packs. We finished by headlamp having lost the sun that winked out its last light at us setting behind the mountain.

I decided to gamble us a more direct route for our return to the gear. But after hiking that course for some time, we ended up in tough, rocky terrain wading through thickets of stunted pines dense with their twisted trunks curled together. Their moisture soaked us. It didn't take long for our packs to feel heavy because they were. The hunter was not doing so hot; we were both falling occasionally on the steep, slippery ground, but when he got up he was labouring pretty hard to do it. As I was leading us, a couple times I emerged through the thickets with a headlamp beam that widened and faded out into the empty and moisture-crystalled air above cliff, steps from my feet. "Don't come this way," I told him before he could see the reason. Sometimes we had to climb up a bit higher before we could try another route back down. Climbing when you're trying to go down can be a morale killer.

A few times we would count off twenty steps, then rest, then twenty more. A mental trick that chunks up the work and helps it to appear more manageable. After a while he called me back in a drained voice. With eyes half shut he said he's struggling, that he dropped some meat. Nothing is truly wasted up there with bears and wolves and foxes and crows, but leaving meat seems dishonourable to the animal and the ethics of hunting. There was zero chance of me turning around for it, though. "Your shoelace." I pointed out to him.

"I can't."

"Hey? You got this man. We're definitely getting closer. We get a cot and fire tonight and sleep in tomorrow. You're doing good. And you got a beautiful animal. Sorry this is so brutal. We have to keep moving, stay with me."

"I can't get it."

He won't drop a knee to tie his boot. I was in my twenties and climbing mountains with weight every day for two months. He was in his forties and gym training only takes you so far. I knelt down and laced up his boot and we hiked on.

We hiked unspeaking in the dark, each of us in our own world with its unique preoccupations and positive voices and negative ones.

At first we didn't notice that it became rare to step with rock underfoot. And then the trees grew taller and the woods opened up. It was easier hiking and we hiked on until we spilled out into the creek bed: our knees silently praising level ground.

"Woooo, yeah buddy!" Soaked in sweat and smiling, I raised arms in victory and looked at him: this man destroyed, just shuffling now on the pebbled ground. "We could make the wall tent in an hour, and not have to set up our tent and cook gear or take it down wet in the morning. We can have a wood fire tonight," I pitched.

"No. No farther. I can't," said the broken man, his headlamp lighting the ground by his boots.

It had been sixteen hours since we started out that morning. "Just one more on level ground takes us to a wood fire." I tried again to sway him.

"No. No way. Sorry."

Right then a good guide would say, "Yeah, fair enough. Good work today." But I really much preferred the zombie walk to base camp rather than setting up, staying here. My last season of fish guiding I was starting to get impatient with the guests, too. It's fair to say my best years of customer service were probably behind me at that point. So after this guy successfully harvested one of the most challenging animals, had paid a lot of money for that privilege, had trained for it, gave it all he had all day working his butt off on this death march I guided him through, I made him feel weak about not hiking one more hour. "Fine, then." I threw a little tantrum and the tent around in setup, mumbled words he didn't hear, a tone he did. The hunter went to bed without eating. I spooned steaming Mountain House beef stroganoff by headlamp in the midnight-quiet and mulled a career change.

THE ALBERMARLE

THE ALBERMARLE WAS THREE STORIES OF RED BRICK with a yellow plaque on its front wall designating it a "Heritage Site." That meant it was old and got no funding. Most that lived there liked it because they were bedbugs; everyone else was less enthused to be staying.

This is an actual review of the Albermarle and I promise I did not write it and have not changed a single thing about it:

Albermarle 1.3 Star Rating. 64 Langside St, Winnipeg Manitoba.

Does this apartment have bed bugs: 2 yes's. 0 No's. Reviewer says . . .

Dirty, smelly from smoke and old stinky walls n carpets never were cleaned.Not cleaned or maintained on regular.I lived there for years and the front door lock was broke all the whole time. Unprofesional landlord and caretaker who ain't got no time for repairs.they ferget about you when they got yer $.they don't ever clean but to rent out to new people & don't do repairs right and cut corners to cost cheaper.Dont expect to be respected and treated decentlee. I ain't ever gonna recommend this place to no one,also it is pigeon infested and health hazard.

Four hundred dollars a month for a one bedroom though, and Todd the landlord didn't tell you about the critters up front. Langside Street started in the North End with the city's highest crime rate, but farther south where we lived it was all right. The Forks and Osborne were only a walk over the bridge or skate down the river under the eyes of the Golden Boy, who my old best bud Andrew with a bundle of wheat and paper-flashlight torch went as for Halloween, me alongside with red Walmart panties over blue tights and a beer-can belt as Duffman. Our hands reddened from high-fives all night a few blocks away at the Winnipeg Convention Centre, its midnight bathroom piss-stunk from drunks hanging it over sinks and garbage cans, where that guy kicked me in my back at the urinal just as big Davey S____, whom I hadn't seen since high school, walked in from a small city of six hundred thousand and handled that for me and whom I never even got to thank because I had to get back to dancing. Thanks, Davey. That evens us up for that time in Grade Two you probably wouldn't remember but I was taking a crap and you climbed up the bathroom stall wall and hung over and had a look at me. Strangely, you now have claim to two poignant bathroom memories. And somehow in a bathroom, you atoned for an offence twenty years prior—*also in a bathroom*. What are the odds?! I love that story! Back to the Albermarle.

One day I was leaving my apartment and I passed a girl in the hallway. *Tight jeans curved body long black parted hair you started it.* I hoped it was her apartment building too and then I didn't see her for a while.

A week or two passed and I know it was Sunday because I was walking back from reading the *Globe and Mail* over a greasy breakfast at the Nook on Sherbrook Street, as I usually did on Sundays. Sometimes I sat long enough I ordered a second breakfast of sausage and eggs and toast and the cook behind the counter liked that. I paid and left for the short walk home on that fall day. Now a half block from the apartment, I turned the corner. Long dark black hair straight down her back. I kept on walking until she climbed the Albermarle's front stairs, and then when the building wall concealed it, I sprinted to close the distance. Making the bottom of the concrete outer stairs, I climbed with fake composure up towards her. I tried to breathe normally, like we'd just happened to arrive at the same time.

"Hey," I said.

"Hey," she said.

She got there first and keyed the door then held it behind her without looking at me.

"If you're the guys living above me I'm gonna keep banging the ceiling with my hockey stick until you settle it down." I knew she didn't live above me but right then it was all I could think to say on the spot to a pretty girl after a sprint before noon.

She laughed a little. "I don't think that's us."

"You're not of the bourgeois class on the top floor?"

"Second."

"Ah. Me too. It's like we're both middle children then."

One single laugh—mine. "I'm Tom."

"Chantelle."

We walked up the wooden stairs whose strip of carpet didn't soften its squeaks, and before Chantelle turned for hers, I asked her number. Between long and dark and straight black parted hair she smiled, and penned it. And briefly, I got her eyes that time.

I called her a day or two later in the late afternoon and she was about to head out but yeah she'll pop over to say hello. Then through the heritage walls that kept few secrets and the floors that echoed them, I heard her coming before she knocked.

She knocked.

"Hey neighbour," I said.

"Hi," her.

She came in and slipped off her slippers and I made a joke about homemade ice and handed her a rye-soda-lime in a crystal tumbler, like the one I was holding too. A Christmas gift set that looked most out of place in a room where she sat down on a grey Value Village couch and me on an orange Value Village recliner.

"So how do you like the Albermarle? Does it live up to its grand name?" I asked.

"Meh. S'all right. I like the location at least." She looked around at the artless walls of a young man living alone.

"I hear ya. The landlord is kind of a turd too."

"Yeah." She pumped my tires every giggle. She told me, "I moved from Transcona, so not so far away, but I was living at home with my mom, wanted a change. My friend Jen was living here with her boyfriend. They split up so I moved in about a month ago."

"That's cool. Okay, yeah, I've seen Jen but I haven't met her. So school, work, what are you doin'?"

"Twenty questions, hey? Geez."

I smiled.

"Well, I've done some photo shoots, some magazines. I've got another in a couple weeks but I'm looking for something else. I was thinking of taking my Early Childhood Educator course. I'd like to work with kids. But I'm only just starting to look into it."

"Nice. I love school. I was at U of M, liberal arts, phil-osophy, English. Took two years of it. Everyone inserts a McDonald's employee joke there, but man I loved it. Loved those courses, the profs, the work, the atmosphere. It was like my own little Enlightenment. I'd work up north in the summers guiding to pay for the winters and so worth it. But yeah, I dunno, I didn't want to teach and not sure if I even could be a prof, so I stopped."

"So, what now?" she asked before the crystal tumbler that had never looked more at home reached her lips.

"And now I'm under the spotlight or what?"

She smiled.

"I got my pilot licence a year ago. But I only did it because I couldn't think of anything else I wanted to do. Didn't want to guide anymore. Had many shitty call centre and construction and odd jobs before that. I was definitely losing my interest in customer service. The fly-ing those pilots did for the lodges I was at seemed like a decent gig so last winter I spent all my oil-rig money, fif-teen grand on aviation school. But it was never my pas-sion like it is for some, just a job really. I'm a bit envious of those people that always knew what they wanted to do, teachers, lawyers, whatever. Never had that. You?"

"Nah, not really either."

"But seems like there'd be some perks for flying as a career anyway. The pay's good after you put your time in. Travel, obviously. This last summer was my first and I flew florts north of Flon Flon. Heh. Tongue twister. Flew. Floats. North of Flin Flon. There we go. Liked it. Almost killed myself a couple times, but liked it. Sometimes I'd drop fishermen off in the morning on a little puddle lake and then take off solo in an empty plane, plug in my MP3 player to my headset and cruise low over trees and rivers and got paid for it. That was pretty sweet. Right now I'm out of St. Andrews on a little wheel plane mostly going back and forth to the reserves, here and Ontario." I started thinking I was talking too much about myself the way pilots probably talk too much about themselves. I asked what her heritage was because I was curious so I asked it.

"My mom's Native, my dad was Italian, is Italian. So why do you have three computer screens?"

"I swear it's not for porn—not just for porn." She laughed, thank God. "I've been playing a little online poker. I've got a friend, a friend of a friend, he's been playing a lot and it's workin' out for him, paying for his school. I've started putting some time into it when I don't have flights. We'll see."

"So, a dropout turned gambler, eh?" she poked.

"Something like that."

I took her glass to refill it without asking, but she stood up to leave. She was my height.

"Gotta run, neighbour," she said, smiling; I don't think I ever stopped.

She slipped on her slippers by the door. I looked at her, raised a closed hand and she pounded it. Then the floorboards creaked little fading laughs at me as I watched her walk away.

A few days passed. I couldn't believe my boss would let me take the plane if I paid for gas on this flightless fall Sunday and holy shit I wondered if she'd say yes.

I called Chantelle and she said just walk over.

"Hi."

"Hi."

"Want to go flying with me for the day? I'm serious. We'll drive out to St. Andrews to the plane. My boss gave me the OK. It's a twenty-minute cruise straight north and we'll go checkout little Gimli for lunch."

"I can't."

"What? Come on."

"Can't."

"Why not? We're going let's go."

"Nooo, I'm scared of flying," she pleaded that out and I believed her.

"Scared of flying or scared of flying with me?"

"Both."

"Hmmm. Suck it up, come on, let's do it. This will ͏appen again. Just fuck it let's go."

ry."

Think. Thinkthinkthink. I sucked in air through my teeth and shook my head. "All riiight. Too bad. Maybe I'll bring you back a cinnamon bun." I racked my brain for anything to change her mind and that was all that rattled out.

I closed her door. The hallway laughed. I closed mine. Then I lay face up on the used couch staring at a ceiling dented from the spearing end of a hockey stick. *Should I go alone? ... Should I call a buddy? ... What else could I say to her without tipping my hand entirely? I want her to come. Hmm.*

This time I didn't hear creaks preceding knocks on the door. I opened.

"Okay," she said.

"Okay, you'll go?"

"Yup. I just gotta do it. But I'm legit scared. I am not happy about this."

The monarch butterflies, just like the Winnipeg retirees, that every fall fly south from the Prairies to warmer places, made a stop in my stomach right then.

"Amazing," I said, and tipped my hand entirely.

I told her nothing of how the small plane would be noisy and bumpy, just to grab her stuff: bathing suit, towel, and we'd leave in an hour.

We drove north to St. Andrews and the quiet Sunday airport. I unlocked the little Cessna 206 on its corner patch of tarmac. We were in and she was buckled safe so I taxied out while talking to the tower, then lined up our runway. Throttle firewalled for takeoff and our plane lifted above an emerging patchwork of farmland, radio towers, rivers, and creeks.

Through headsets, my inquiry: "Are you okay?"

She nodded and thumbs-upped and I asked if she wanted to fly and she thumbs-downed and I laughed and we were good.

With the ocean of Lake Winnipeg growing on the horizon I broadcasted our position as we approached the unmanned little airport, then touched down smooth its runway.

We walked the few shops. There actually was a good bakery and we did get cinnamon buns to take to the beach. But fall's cool temps and grey skies above lake made its water uninviting even to a guy with a pretty girl holding a bag with a bathing suit. "Well, that was wishful thinking," I said and she laughed.

We sat on the beach, tore pieces from the buns that rained odd drops of raisins and walnuts. I pounded Lake Winnipeg's fine sand.

"Pretty, though," I said.

"Beautiful," her.

I crab-walked my hand over the sand towards her, flicked sand onto her hand, and then crab-walked it back to me.

"This will sound super obvious but to me it's still something weird what a plane does to perspective. You fly up over the trees and things become defined, the properties and boundaries are squared, organized, everything's smaller. It's sorta strange, right? Or does that sound stupid or something only a kid would find interesting? It's crazy to think you could be in Afghanistan or Iraq if you wanted to in a few hours. In hours, today, you could be in a war zone or a famine. You see things on TV and they seem like different worlds. They still burn people alive as witches every year in parts of Kenya, and if you leave early you could be there in a day. It's like you're flying back in time. That's just astounding to me. That's how close it is. Like to me it seems that should be a lot harder to get to. A month of travel. But it's not. That's weird."

Chantelle unspeaking threw a stone towards the lake.

"Man, it's just something else here. Canada is something else. It's truly lucky to be born here and not Afghanistan or somewhere. I'm not a thirteen-year-old girl getting battery acid thrown in my face for trying to read before I'm sold into slave marriage. I can say those words but not even process what that really means. I actually do feel like I could do anything. Start a company. Run one. Run for parliament—I know that sounds cheesy, but I do. It's like you live here and it's all on the table, y'know? That's pretty incredible. I can go to the oil rigs with no education and make a hundred grand a year. Are you kidding me? Where else can you do that? Maybe nowhere else. That's something. Effort matters and sometimes it pays in full, sometimes more. I love that." I said it and meant it.

"That's cool," she said and laughed a little. "Must be nice."

"Yeah," I said. "It is."

We sat beside each other and we both looked out at the big water: an uncaring thing. Not mean—*indifferent*. Its potential joys and punishments. It could pay; it could demand payment. It could take different shapes. Two people could look at it and see two different things at the same time and both were true.

"Do you think you wake up with that feeling? Just pull yourself up by your bootstraps?" she asked.

I thought on it. "No."

"Things look a little different for some. If your family does it differently. *If* a mom and dad. If your aunties and uncles . . . Sometimes you see what you're shown. A lot of people I know didn't finish high school. Sometimes family doesn't want you going away from home all the time to jobs or school or whatever. They like you close. You like it too. Sometimes there's other things too that make it hard. Y'know it's not on the table for everyone. Not the same anyway. But that sounds nice. I mean that,

that's not sarcasm. What you said actually sounds really nice for you, Tom. Just sometimes it's a little different and not so far away either," said Chantelle.

"I get it."

"Yeah?" she smiled.

Seagulls and their sounds. Boats on the water. Fresh smell of a lake. You've seen it before and it's nice. We zipped our hoodies and our bare feet laid twin paths on cold sand while our voices and laughter lapped the shore.

Then evening came and again our Cessna lifted. We headed south for the flight home and our heads turned to the orange glow of a sunset whose same light right then was lighting up other places where those monarchs went and Afghans are and Winnipeggers are and Tla-o-qui-aht are and Tofitians are and we were.

By the night we were back at her place and a flickering candle made bright her face and light on her lips and the little gold in her eyes were like keyholes bursting light and my hand at the end of her knee over her jeans I leaned to kiss her, high on her smell doing it. So close there was warmth too. Her straight long black hair parted and hanging like curtains. And then she smiled, and she laughed just a little.

BEARDED ANGELS

THERE ARE TWO TYPES OF NEAR-DEATH EXPERIENCE. The more common is the type we are oblivious to: the stone our bike tire nearly rides over that would have sent us falling into traffic, the replicating cell our immune system almost fails to kill. Unseen coin flips of tragedy. But there are those experiences whose immediacy we are fully aware of, whose horror-shock have our full attention. This story is one of those.

I was flying a turbo-charged 206 float plane near the northern border of Manitoba. A Cessna 206 is often described unfavourably as a dog in the air. But unloaded and turbo-charged, at least it was a dog with a rocket strapped to its ass.

I had just finished dropping off a load of motors to a vacant outpost cabin, then pushed myself off from the dock on the calm water and taxied empty out to the middle of the lake. A windless day meant I could pick any direction for takeoff and a round body of water meant it was all the same anyways. I flowed through my mental checklist: *flaps, undercarriage, rudders, doors, load secure, checkcheckcheckcheckcheck.* I enriched the mixture, full-throttled power, and as I built speed, gently pulled the steering back to coax her up on plane. It took a long time to get there and then when I tried to ease her off the water into air, we were stuck to the surface. The speed increasing, still no lift. This was the same method I'd done hundreds of times and the plane always took flight. *Why not now?* I didn't know what was going on and the shore was getting closer. *She always lifts, always, lifts, lift-liftliftliftlift, come on.* I stared out at the rapidly increasing size of a large immovable object that was the Canadian shore. *Lift.* Nothing.

I debated what to do: *Pull power, lose my speed and start over? Or give it a second and fly away?* In that moment I saw no reason to pull power because the plane had a fast airspeed, was unloaded, and always, always lifts. *Ahhh, I'm not in a hurry, okay.* I killed the power. I cannot stress enough how haphazardly, how casually, I came to that decision. *That was the most important single decision I've knowingly made in my entire life.* Another day I would absolutely not have cut the engine.

But with the speed I'd built, the plane's forward momentum didn't stop and I tore down the lake and closed in on the big forest. There was nothing I could think to do. I couldn't turn at this speed, but I did consider just trying to steer into one and taking the resultant flip and roll on the water, instead of a crash in the bush. I debated my options with the speed of a mind jacked on neurotransmitters jumping gaps like electric thoroughbreds. My mind was not on lovers or family or pretty words or foul ones: it was just running through options—and none of them seemed good.

About a hundred feet in front of me I saw the pale white of a reef under the surface. That distance closed in an instant, and with the timpani and bass notes of rocks on aluminum pontoons: I hit. The plane banged and bounced and screeched like nails on chalkboard up onto the shallow sunken rocks. And that's where I stopped. And that's me sitting seatbelted in, headset on, staring through the cockpit windshield at a forest that always knew victory in our game of chicken. It was modest in victory: everything was enormously, juxtaposingly quiet now.

The air did not smell like fuel nor did I hear the tinkle of water filling my floats. *Good signs.* I got out of the plane still wondering what the hell happened. I noticed my flaps were not down: said them in my checklist, did not finger their switch. This was one hundred percent user error. "Whoops," I said to myself. Looking down I couldn't believe the floats weren't shredded. A couple dents, but they looked okay. I imagined there were gaping holes on the bottom, though—how could there not be? But the undercarriage looked intact and true, and I was incredulous.

Well, now what? I stepped my boots down onto the reef in ankle-deep water. I laid my shoulder against the strut supporting a wing. Well braced, I took some deep breaths, and set to push that fucker free into the water. She tilted up a bit: the farther wing lowered and the nearest rose. But she remained unconvinced. I tried different iterations of lifting angles and curse words hoping I could find the perfect combination to push this bird off the reef. But none of them did the trick. *What would Fred do?*

There was a hatchet in the cabin of the plane and I waded with that to shore and hacked down a pine. Returning with my twenty-foot-long fresh-cut and carpentered lever, for just a minute, just a sweet single minute, I felt a little clever there. That's the resiliency of my ego: even after crashing a perfectly good plane on a calm day without a load seemed like a fine time to sneak in a little patting of the back. Anyways, I wedged one end of that log between pontoon and bedrock, waded to its other end suspended in the air above the reef, heaved my weight onto wood, and watched that plane stay right where it was. "Rats."

I sat on the float in the sun and had a snack and a brainstorm session but nothing came. Soon someone was going to realize I wasn't where I was supposed to be and get worried. I wasn't ashamed of the situation; if you talk to any bush pilot they'd be able to tell you of many times they had close calls. It's inevitable in that profession due to weather and mechanical issues and simply pilot error. It happens. It was my fault, but it happens. Eventually you'll find yourself in a pickle. And so I was in one. However, who would want to literally broadcast their screw up to anyone that happened to be listening on the radio at that moment? With a deep and reluctant sigh, I got on the radio. I didn't mayday, I just sorta probed. I knew the other pilot working for the hunting lodge I was contracted for was flying somewhere near this same route.

"Eligh, you on here?"

Radio silence.

There was no civilization around, not much bush plane traffic either, and my signal didn't carry far at this low elevation. I said his plane's call sign and my call sign.

"Go ahead," he responded. *Amazing.*

I brought him up to speed with as few details as possible, just enough for him to get the picture. I spoke my location and he wasn't far off.

There is a consistent theme to my life of horseshoes stuck in private places. Within the hour, Eligh landed his plane on my lake. He touched down, taxied over. I don't expect anyone to believe this but it's truth: the cargo that loaded his Beaver was *four burly moose hunters with hip waders.* I promise. These bearded angels put hands on the fuselage, Eligh on the strut, Archimedes mostly embarrassed of his predicament but a tiny bit proud of his lever, and three two one in unison we heaved and lifted and popped her unstuck from the rock and free to float! My Cessna 206 howdareanyonecallheradog *did not sink.*

Back in the cockpit now, I started her up, idled her around, tested the controls and steering and listened to the putter of the engine sounding healthy. I checklisted including flaps this time, firewalled that fucking throttle and she responded with a pure and loud roar followed by wicked acceleration of the turbo charger. Steering eased back from my pull, I coaxed her up to plane on the water. And a short sweet second later, *she and I lift.* And I'm up and away and over the reef and over the boulders and over the trees and I'm smiling and I'm yelling and I'm singing to myself.

DIRTY SECRETS

THE AVIATION WORLD HAS A FEW DIRTY LITTLE SECRETS. Here's one: if you're being flown by a first-year pilot, the owners are paying him or her little, paying the insurance companies a lot, crossing their fingers he or she doesn't crash the plane and kill himself/herself/others, and with the hopes of getting a few good flying years out of that pilot before he or she tries to make money out of this career choice.

Here's another: sometimes pilots are pressured to fly overloaded planes beyond what the aeronautical engineers designed the plane to carry and made clear in the owner's manual but it's hard to get your start as a pilot with no experience and why would they want to crash their own plane so you'll say okay and barely make it over the trees and curse that guy.

One more: as a passenger, sometimes you'll look out the window and see the world blown up with strong winds, trees aslant, and heavy tall black clouds on the horizon, and you'll look over at your young bush pilot who'll look calm and will calmly say to you, "We're going to divert to this small grass-strip not too far away and let the storm pass over us." And he'll smile, and then if you keep watching you'll see him push the throttle right to max right to the firewall and his knuckles are white and he hasn't let go of the throttle. And everything is fine.

B____ was the former chief of a small reserve in Northern Ontario. Like many of those reserves, there were no roads in, no boat access, just small plane transport. He had his pilot licence, owned a small aviation company, including a Cessna 206 on wheels and a turbine Otter on amphibious floats. I flew for him for one season. After I had gotten the job, someone told me if you shake hands with him, count all your fingers afterwards. But at that time I didn't know it and it's hard to find flying gigs as a pilot with low hours. He hired me and I was grateful.

On a wintry Manitoban afternoon, I was flying a couple passengers from just north of Winnipeg, from St. Andrews, my point of departure and town that raised me. Besides their luggage, the cargo was a bit of food, and KFC and pop. Our destination was a small northern reserve near the Manitoba-Ontario border.

I spotted the frozen ice runway, determined the winds, reduced power, dropped my flaps, and then touched down on the rough surface. It takes a bit longer to reduce speed on ice rather than tarmac, and so I continued to steadily apply the brakes. As we bumped along the runway, I noticed that ahead of us, someone had drilled an ice-fishing hole. If you drilled it on the cleared-off runway as opposed to any other part of the lake, you didn't have to shovel the snow first—I get that.

You can't turn a plane that's just landed and going fast on any surface. Also, you don't dodge things. I was curious how this would play out, and right then my role was spectator. But the same God that forsook His own son who was also Himself; the One who was deaf to the prayers of six million Jews He called His own people; who turned His back on Dostoyevsky's little girl beating her tiny fist against her chest in the filth; who watched the slaughters of Hutus Tutsis Cambodians Vietnamese Russians First Peoples the world over; the Creator of cancers; Architect of famines; Skinner of knees; and whose Earth is saturated with tears from crust to core, gracefully granted us safe passage that day on the ice: the fishing hole slipping between the wheels. I wondered two things: Would it have just taken out a tire? And did he catch any fish?

If I were to ask you where the highest suicide rates per capita in the world are, reasonable responses might be Afghanistan or South Sudan or the downtown core of major developed countries. And all of those would be wrong. Turns out it is small and isolated Northern Canadian communities, also known as ancestral villages, also known as reserves.

I heard B____ and his son would fly up to a lake close to that isolated community with a load. You don't land at the town, just close. And a boat driven by a friend from the village would come and meet them. The price you could get was high if it was a "dry" reserve. This is a place where the people in their struggle against the challenges of addiction in small towns with little work and modest education and poor diets and where they can't always drink the water had decided to pass a bylaw to forbid the sale of alcohol—something that just wasn't working for them. But that's where you could get the highest price for it. Right, B____?

FIRST OF THE LOST

IT WAS COLD OUTSIDE AND IT WAS BEAUTIFUL OUTSIDE and I was only outside because it was beautiful. It also smelled nice. The stars were out in full and I could see their glitter through cedar needles. When I bought the place there was a shed there, set back from the house, and it once held chickens—and I tore it down and built a shed that holds chickens. It's got one of the best spots on the property. There's a big magnolia tree that doesn't bloom until late summer and when it does, with its banana leaves and velvet undersides, the big blooming ivory petals don't look real and you can smell it when you open the backdoor that's nowhere close. There're a couple rhodos as there are everywhere in this town where some people think theirs are most special but mine stand well overhead and bloom in big drooping arches and are. There's a hydrangea I think I killed—but we have other things on our mind tonight.

I gave a good search, and now in this last hour I stopped looking because she'd been in the wild company of minks and martens and snakes and eagles and dogs and cats for too long. I just hope it was quick. I shouldn't have let you guys out and this is why I don't. I know she used to all the time, but we've now passed into the era of the patriarch.

At least the rest of the little family came back chirping and peeping and clucking. Whole flocks get massacred when a mink squeezes its tiny head through a chink in the coop. And you can't really seal off all the attack vectors; if they can break out of Alcatraz they can break into this. Or something will burrow, tunnel its way into the run. And with that creative talent and long-term vision our enemy deserves our respect if not our admiration. It may be inevitable. But this chick was the first of the lost and that's not too bad. I'll keep a watch over you girls. And we've been snapping rat necks and stacking bodies like it's a military coup—*wartime crimes, girls, I'm your soldier.*

There was enough moonlight and starlight out I could see to wander the familiar ground: under the magnolia, past the evergreen huckleberry and compost, under the rhodos, back behind the coop, beside the bedrock hill with its cedar trees of modest height growing up out of it.

My eyes casually followed channels of bark up one of the trunks, passing knots and knobs of lower branches I'd trimmed, up into its height. And there: *masked eyes—I saw the face of a bandit.* His body angled away from me but his head cocked my direction. He was wide-eyed alert and had clearly been watching me soliloquize like a crazy person. We traded stares with the disquiet of both of our privacies invaded. And then my posture tightened at the thought — *His presence: coincidence or otherwise?*

I scanned for downy little fluff caught between his whiskers like snowflakes. I considered telling him a joke and if he smiled I'd look to see if his teeth were stained with the blood of the innocent. I had to corral my prejudice and remind myself the gods painted him a guilty face. I considered shooting him, but that seemed cruel and inglorious and not of the rules of engagement these critters and I tacitly signed up for; an invading army of rats is one thing, this little unarmed bastard in the tree is another. While I looked into the black pools of his eyes to divine if the sins of this King of Rodents befell my flock, I knew he was simultaneously trying to window my thoughts to decide if he should roll the dice and chuck himself into a twenty-foot freefall, or continue trading stares with a psycho and wait for me to make the first move. It was tense.

I looked in the direction his body faced. Down on the bedrock in a small salal patch between ivy vines poked a blonde baby head. *The MIA.* She was dead still. She blinked. *She's alive.* I swooped in before he pounced and extracted her then turned without looking again at the enemy and we retreated to the shed where the heavy door closed behind us. A brood reunited celebrated with chirps and peeps and clucks and fuckyeahs safe behind the wire walls for another night.

THE TIRES

ALL COUPLES HAVE SPATS NOW AND AGAIN. MAYBE A few don't but we're not all living fairy tales. What does their timeline really matter? If they happen early you can learn more about each other early. Instead of treading lightly with some hidden land mines down the road, you get lucky and a few go off sooner. Now you know your breaking points. How is that not preferable? Maybe even couples counselling early if it comes to that—you shore up your foundation early, you build this thing properly, professionally, if it came to that.

He came home from work one day and she was gone. They were together for a while, long enough for her to move in, not long enough for a brother to cross provinces and meet her. He texted that time when they were in the car on a road trip together. It sounded bad. But when it was good it must have been really good because he said he had bought a ring.

The early evening light came in through the big living room window, but he flicked the switch out of habit.

Overhead, the bulbs remained unlit. The house seemed cold because it was. He saw the naked walls where once hung photos and paintings, their bareness shocking. And if they had bought it together, she had taken it. Even some things that were clearly his, some tools, were gone as well.

He walked from room to room and took in the sight of bare shelves, of closet space, of empty hangers. Every room was cold and none of the lights worked either and that was odd. The electrical panel showed no breakers had been thrown. He made his way out to the garage and noticed she had not taken her summer tires that were mounted on rims and stacked in the corner.

An electrician came the next day, and from inside a wall socket, he found a clipped wire and an obstruction: a folded-up piece of paper. He read it and passed it along. There were insults with poor spelling, and the note had the mark of idiocy that would be hard to surpass. Her brother, an electrician, had signed his name at the bottom.

The imaginative cruelty to take a home that so recently housed love within its walls, steal from it, and then shut off its power in winter, is exclusively unique to humankind. It's one of those things that separates us from the wild animals in the forests. To sign one's name to the crime is something particularly special.

A few days later she texted him with instructions to leave the forgotten tires at the end of the driveway and she and her brother would come by to pick them up. So now he called his own brother and there began the strategizing of what to do with these expensive tires. You could say, *They weren't there, didn't see them.* And they'd be yours. But her brother was an idiot so you'd have to think about putting up cameras 'cause there might be backlash. Slashing them seemed unimaginative, cliché. At least deflate them? You could sell them online, use the money to recoup what was paid to the electrician and for the stolen tools; if there was any money left, she could have it. That seemed entirely fair and reasonable. With many options on the table, he said he'd think on it.

Later that week he carried the tires out one by one from the garage and walked them to the end of the driveway. He stacked them up. He left a note. Here's what it read: *Let me know if you need a hand putting them on.*

This also seems particularly unique to humankind.

IN HER DAY

MY GRANDMA LOIS WAS NOW OLD: FRAIL AND HUNCH-
ing and shuffling, sometimes lost in thought or lacking
it. And do you even know what dementia is when you're
diagnosed? Is it a fog bank that never lifts, or like cloud
cover with vision between?

One Christmas, one of her last, her daughter flew
to Winnipeg to bring her back to Calgary for Christmas. Lois's son and daughter-in-law, my dad and mom,
who lived in Winnipeg, would fly out to Calgary later.
Both families, with wives and husbands and children and
grandchildren, would spend an evening together.

The house had been decorated, and the tree. There
was a big turkey dinner, wine poured for those that
wanted. We all caught up, told stories and laughed. There
were desserts with coffee. Later into the evening, the two
families were sitting in the living room together with
Christmas music in the background, and small or large
conversations spanning the chairs and couches.

Someone gave Lois a Santa hat with a white fleece
band, soft red felt, and a little bell on top. Her daughter,

who loved her, encouraged her to stand up in the space that formed in the middle. That daughter held her mom's shrivelled soft and veiny hands and Lois, while standing there, bent her knees and bobbed in place just a bit, turned slightly from side to side. *A little dance.* Her grey hair curled out and under the Santa hat her glasses held up. And the little bell jingled like Christmas.

Lois's son, who brought Lois her weekly groceries, took her to church, drove her out to St. Andrews for dinners, her son who would take her to the doctors, who would later help clothe her, who would later help lift her off the apartment floor, knew that only a year or two ago she would never behave this way. How she'd be mortified if she realized what she was doing right now in front of everyone. He could feel her embarrassment for her, maybe a touch of shame in not stopping it or towards the others revelling in it. And the word itself so disgraceful, something you could only think, not say, maybe later whisper: *clown.*

With everyone now watching, the daughter would pass off her mother's hands to the next person beside. And they would now hold *dancing Lois.*

In her day, before her grandchildren, Lois danced with Mel. I never met him. Mel took her to the town fairs and the socials, the occasional celebrations of small-town Stonewall, Manitoba. I heard she loved nothing more and that they could both dance, that people would watch them.

Then in the space between the chairs and couches, with music softly playing, Lois let go a hand. And the other. In the middle of her family, a family that had distances and disconnections not uncommon to families, but in the middle of her family nonetheless, she bent her knees and bobbed in place just a bit, she turned slightly from side to side. And she was absolutely, radiantly, smiling.

EVOLUTION

IF I SAID THIS HAPPENED THE WINTER EVERYONE WENT to Mexico and La Perouse buoy stopped working and one of your friends moved away and your other friends got pregnant and you forgot that Co-Op closed early and you forgot that the hardware store closed on Sundays and I was up on the roof trying to stop a leak when it rained like a son of a bitch and the town lost power and you made love and surf water spilled out of your nose on your lover—that would not help because that was all of them.

We were down at the Weigh West. Or maybe it was the Way West—that always made more sense to me. The pub anyways. Before it was Jacks Jacks Jacks, before it was the Hatch. We were a few drinks in and it wasn't late, but we were calling it a night anyways. We headed outside through the big wooden doors where some of our friends walked left to go home towards Crab Dock, and some got on bikes for other routes. My route would take me up the hill and then right for the walk through town to the Tibbs.

John and I started off together from the pub doors, then he made a turn to the docks for a jet ski home to the floathouse.

"Woah, buddy. You're not driving that thing after putting a few back," I told him.

"I only had two. I'm good. Thanks, though."

"Tss-nah. Can't let you do it. I better go with you."

"Uhh, okay then," John replied.

I had never been on a jet ski. I did, however, come from years of riding snowmobiles on the prairies with its tides and currents most predictable. Those skills would translate well, I figured. It's fair to say that right then my heart was pure, my logic flawed.

We opened up Trilogy, the store he owned beside the docks, and swapped out my Blundstones for the rubber boots of one of his staff—they're rubber boots in Manitoba, they're gumboots here; some habits die hard. We walked down the ramp, John started the sea-whip, and I saddled up. Immediately, we almost tipped at the dock. *Okay, nothing like my Ski-Doo, more like a canoe. The Red River, the Bloodvein, I'm well-travelled by paddle. No problem.*

"Good, here." And I double-tapped his waist.

He twisted the throttle to give her some gas, one of us burped like he was blowing on the dice Evolution here was about to roll. And we took off.

Our wake in the harbour. Our wake hitting Straw-berry. Wind and rain in our hair, feeling like a good friend with my hands on the hips of my buddy. Now seconds from seeing the floathouse, we curved into the gap between Riley and Neilson.

The motor coughed. The motor quit.

The sound of a jet ski in the harbour is an assault on many things. The silence when its engine unexpectedly dies is Nature licking her finger and marking up a win.

It's calm and quiet, and we bob and drift.

"What the hell," we both thought, and someone said.

As we tilted to one side, I was surprised at how hard it was for two people to balance on an unmoving jet ski. And with that, very slowly, very bravely, we completed our roll into the water.

The water took our breath away like Evolution, her cold-hearted self, just hoofed us in the groin. It was spring and the ocean was still winter-cold, and this spot between the islands and the rocks was full of cur-rent. Alcohol. No life jackets. Our jet ski was starting to be pulled by the current and away from us, while rubber boots, filling with water and heavy, slowed our front crawl to a crawl—but it's easy to send a good pair of Dunlops to the bottom when they're not yours. John kicked his off too. And sock-footed now we paddled eas-ily for that shitty vessel. The slick rubber of our Helly

Hansens glided through the water like the bodies of two extremely motivated but mentally challenged harbour seals.

We caught up and held to our Sea-Doo drifting in the rain. John climbed up and then I did. And then we tilted and fell again. Physics says we couldn't both stay on without the momentum from its forward motion making it minorly more stable. So right then and quickly, we hashed out the plan. Stage One: John gets back up, fires it alive if she'll go. Stage Two: I hang on and off the back and ski my body until we have enough speed to support my climb and hold my sit.

Stage One was a go and we executed flawlessly. I was now being pulled behind our water-rocket with a well-sobered face full of exhaust and ocean spray. John drove on. I pulled and climbed: I was up. If Evolution was listening to my thoughts at that moment, she'd have heard that *my haters inspire me.*

"Nice," I say.

For John and me right then the world felt very keen and very alive. Wind and rain once again in our hair. The entire harbour again alerted to the sound of our craft. We rounded the turn past Riley, shot the gap by Morpheus like a couple of Neos; the green floathouse walls now in sight.

Then Evolution said, "Round Two." The motor coughed. And the motor quit.

"Fucksake." We rolled into the water.

But now we were sock-footed seasoned pros. Unspeaking, we exchanged glances and nods. Short seconds later we were back up. Not many more and we docked that son of a bitch. And John and I, elated to be alive, slapped hands and yelled and commended ourselves.

WONDERMENT

RETA GREW UP ON A FARM IN MANITOBA AND WITH thirteen siblings. There was musical talent among them and sometimes in the evenings and after the crops were harvested in the fall, the family would play the fiddle and harmonica, guitar, banjo, and spoons and she loved it. She herself could tickle the ivories and kept a piano in the house for decades.

We celebrated Gran's ninetieth birthday a couple years ago. This was not a celebration where the lady of honour was physically present but mentally absent, no, Gran at ninety was sharp, interesting, well spoken and well written. She could not only walk but dance too, albeit slowly, and when I asked her for one, saying I'd do my best not to step on her toes, she accepted.

Gran opened presents and blew out candles. Under strung garland and floating balloons, a room outfitted for the birthday party of our favourite nonagenarian, we celebrated into the evening. Food was catered, cake was served, and she had a slice with her glass of sherry. One of my uncles narrated a slideshow with scenes of youthful times, Grandad before and after the war, children and grandchildren.

Into the evening her daughter-in-law and a grand-daughter sang and played guitar and fiddle. Some that knew the words joined in, and Gran too while she tapped out the rhythm on her lap.

I heard in an interview someone say that over his long life he always had something that got him up in the morning, something that got him excited about the day to unfold. In part, he credited that anticipation for living a long life. This is not a novel concept, but it was the first time I heard it named: "Wonderment."

Last year I asked Gran a few questions by email, and at ninety-three, on her own personal computer and with grammar far better than mine, her response:

> I believe good health and longevity is partly determined by the genes we inherit from our parents, partly how we care for our bodies, and greatly by our mental attitude and our approach to life. Anticipation factors into it, too. This may sound silly but each Christmas Judy renews my subscription to the *Calgary Herald* and it is delivered to my door by six a.m. I can scarcely wait to sit down with it before breakfast (served at eight a.m.) and begin (trying) to solve the crossword along with all the other puzzles

on the page. I enjoy going down to the dining room for breakfast and being greeted by all the other "early" risers. To answer your questions:

No, I do not drink coffee at all, though I did at one time. It just no longer appeals to me, so now I have my cup of green tea, but one of these days I'm going to try the Red Rose brand as it seems to be a favourite with so many—even the Queen, I understand.

Sleep? I often take naps in the aft as I do have difficulty falling asleep, even though I enjoy going to bed. For some reason my mind won't shut down and allow me to slumber in the arms of Morpheus.

My diet? The chef serves good balanced meals considering how many palates he has to satisfy, and I make a point of eating the garnishes—celery leaves, kale, etc. My iron intake! We often have fish—but overcooked I fear.

You flatter me, Tom, with regard to my mental sharpness, but thanks.

My love to you and Ashley,

Gran xxoo

Whether or not it's tea and crosswords, to approach a century of life and still wake with exuberance for pleasures so simple as the morning paper is a type of large fortune. I think back to this email sometimes. What matters and what doesn't. Sift wheat from chaff. Find wonderment.

EPILOGUE

I HOPE THESE STORIES AREN'T SELF-AGGRANDIZING and don't glorify or politicize or moralize much. They're mostly a small and personal bit of Canadiana. They're memories and history. Not history like the pyramids, just some of my own. Maybe they've had the wash and fill of time, the gloss of nostalgia, but they ring true in my ears. Some things, I regret. There's no pride, just history—the cold and the broken and the beautiful too. All of it holy.

NOTES

IN THE STORY "SHORE-LUNCH MEMORIES," I SAID "[Jimmy] pitched high on the *o* then hung to it with a sound made through teeth gone missing like the buildings in North End, Winnipeg [. . .]." This line is similar to the lyrics from the song "Left and Leaving" from the Winnipeg-based band The Weakerthans: "My city's still breathing, but barely, it's true, through buildings gone missing like teeth."

BIBLIOGRAPHY

1. Hanson, Erin. "The Residential School System,"
    Indigenous Foundations, accessed March 3, 2020,
    https://indigenousfoundations.arts.ubc.ca/
    the_residential_school_system/.

2. Schwartz, Daniel. "Truth and Reconciliation
    Commission: By the numbers," *CBC*, published
    June 2, 2015, https://www.cbc.ca/news/indigenous/
    truth-and-reconciliation-commission-by-the-
    numbers-1.3096185.

ABOUT THE AUTHOR

TOM STEWART WAS BORN IN 1982 AND GREW UP IN St. Andrews north of Winnipeg. He attended University of Manitoba taking literature and philosophy for two years, dropped out, and worked across Northern Canada as a fishing and hunting guide, oil-rig roughneck, bush pilot, and he backpacked internationally in the off-seasons. Tom played poker for several years, no longer flies planes, and now lives in Tofino, Vancouver Island. UNDERBIGHEARTEDSKIES.COM

The book market is a competitive place especially for new authors. Reviews help. If you liked any of the stories, please write a review at Amazon, Indigo, Barnes and Noble, or wherever you purchased the book. Thanks.

—Tom

Made in the USA
Las Vegas, NV
08 December 2020

12331737R00135